Jaroslav Kusnír (Ed.)

Ideology and Aesthetics in American Literature and Arts

Jaroslav Kusnír (Ed.)

Ideology and Aesthetics in American Literature and Arts

ibidem-Verlag
Stuttgart

Bibliografische Information Der Deutschen Bibliothek

Die Deutsche Bibliothek verzeichnet diese Publikation in der Deutschen Nationalbibliografie; detaillierte bibliografische Daten sind im Internet über <http://dnb.ddb.de> abrufbar.

∞

Gedruckt auf alterungsbeständigem, säurefreien Papier
Printed on acid-free paper

ISBN: 3-89821-513-X

Printed in Germany

TABLE OF CONTENTS

INTRODUCTION

Ideology and Aesthetics in Literature

Jaroslav Kušnír

Many contemporary theories (some feminist and post-colonial theories, Marxism) emphasize ideological rather than artistic, literary and aesthetic values of literary texts. According to Richard Levin,

"'ideology' refers to a consciously held set of beliefs or creed, usually in the social or political realm. In this sense ideological approach to Shakespeare would be one that is deliberately constructed from such a creed in order to serve it, and the two most important examples today are Marxist and feminist criticism" (Levin 1996: 138).

As can be seen from this extract, the ideological approach to literary texts is not interested in their intrinsic aesthetic and literary quality, uniqueness of style or poetics, or in the way these refer to particular social reality, but in the way ideology is expressed regardless the aesthetic value of the signifier. Thus it follows that a work of art is important only to the extent it expresses certain ideological views, class or racial conflict as manifestations of these positions. From the perspective of these theories, a literary work is not always understood and researched in its entirety as a phenomenon able to convey human experience through the authors' use of original style, narrative techniques and, more generally, artistic "language." The focus of critics and theorists defending ideologically and sociologically biased theories, as indicated above, is often restricted to analysis of fashionable terms and phenomena such as race, gender, class or ethnicity. A literary work is thus understood as a cultural, sociological or politological document equal to any other "discourses". In such an understanding, it loses its specificity as an artistic and aesthetic artifact bearing unique features, that is the features that are able to express a unique vision of the world specific for particular cultures, gender, class or ethnic identities. Each literary work represents an outer, physical reality and experience through the specific use of the signifier, the "language" which is different from the language of sociological, legal or any other documents. Early in the 20th century, despite their overestimation of literary language, the Formalists, and the New Critics later, identified a uniqueness and specificity of literary language finding it different from any other languages, styles and discourses. This approach focusing on the analysis of the language and narrative strategies of a literary work seems to be relevant for understanding of the nature of literature, since whatever different literary theories and approaches to the literary text may claim, it is evident that literary text refers to outer reality through specific use of language. That is why the study of this language, its reference to reality and its creation of meaning can provide us, along with the study of particular social and historical contexts, with the understanding of the creation of meaning related to particular social and cultural contexts. Thus the understanding of a literary text and its relation to external reality requires understanding of the literary language used by particular authors to convey a message about external, physical experience and the social world. Language becomes a tool and a bridge by means of which authors try to overcome barriers and distance between the perception of the world and its representation, between language and reality, between the mental process of association of ideas and the materiality of language representing it. As Charles Newman argues,

"Language is 'given', a phenomenon which is neither autonomous 'nor' coextensive with our lives. And literature, thus, is a gift— not the property of a class or even an individual prophet— a present, which, like all exemplary endowments, creates its own terms of acceptance" (Newman 1985: 97).

And Newman further continues that

"[...]we should recall that fiction always exists in a double sense: as reports on changing patterns of human behaviour, as well as on the evolution of forms[...]Literature is not a religion, or philosophy, or psychology, it is not a political act, or intrinsically virtuous, neither weapon nor sanctuary; least of all is it therapy" (96-97).

Ideological, politological, and sociological study of a literary work means a study of the objects of physical reality and social relationships, that is of the signified rather than a signifier, during the process of which language loses the uniqueness of its aesthetic function. With such an approach, language is understood as a clear, rational but unimportant mediator of the external world corresponding almost to physical reality, and rather a mechanic tool transferring the data through language. In other words, physical reality, physical objects and phenomena become the measure of all things that are inseparable from the language. A literary work (its language) thus becomes understood as the same object as the objects it represents, that is language becomes reality. This means then that a literary work is deprived of its aesthetic function, that is of a quality which forms the ontological basis of literature itself. What is misunderstood here is the working of two different principles, versions of reality and ontological systems. As Paul de Man argues,

"Literature is fiction not because it somehow refuses to acknowledge 'reality,' but because it is not 'a priori' certain that language functions according to principles which are those, or which are 'like' those, of the phenomenal world [...]

It would be unfortunate, for example, to confuse the materiality of the signifier with the materiality of what it signifies" (De Man 1982:11).

Paul de Man even understands the confusion of linguistic with natural reality as ideology (De Man 1982: 11). The approach of the sociological, ideological and political critics makes any analysis of a literary work ideological, political and sociological, irrespective of the literary and aesthetic values of these texts. Among the most significant ideological approaches to literary texts is Marxist analysis, and the approaches deriving their critical instruments from it (some feminist and post-colonial theories). Dealing with the theories of the naturalization of narrative texts, Mas'ud Zavarzadeh calls such theories neo-mimetic and he argues that

"[...]they see the work of art as a way of recoding the existing version of reality as formulated in various patterns of verisimilitude. They also simplify the act of reading by suggesting a move from the text,

admittedly with some complication, to the world" (Zavarzadeh 1985: 624-625).

Keith Green and Jill LeBihan further suggest that

"With Marxism we never forget that 'literature' and texts are the products of a specific class and are materially produced at points in history, being determined by factors other than divine or poetic grace"(Green, LeBihan 1996: 124).

And the ideological, political and sociological position of a feminist approach can be clearly seen from C. Weedon's words: *"Feminism is a politics. It is a politics directing at changing existing power relations between women and men in society"* (Weedon 1987:1). Some years later, a very similar position can be found in Catherine Belsey's and J. Moore's feminist anthology entitled typically *The Feminist Reader: Essays in Gender and the Politics of Literary Criticism:*

"The feminist reader is enlisted in the process of changing the gender relations which prevail in our society, and she regards the practise of reading as one of the sites in the struggle for change" (Belsey and Moore 1989:1).

Despite many literary works' cliché-like character, social and ideological bias, and their authors' lack of artistic mastery, with the ideological approaches many works are understood as good and valuable only because they deal to a certain extent with either class, ethnic or gender identity. Examples of the success of ideology but failure of aesthetic and artistic values may be some works and short stories by the South African novelist Nadine Gordimer (albeit a Nobel prize winner), the novel by British-Pakistani author Hannif Kureishi *My Beautiful Laundrette*, or contemporary Chinese-American author Anchee Min's novel *Wild Ginger* (2002). These novels were critically highly acclaimed for their depiction of interracial (post-colonial), minority (ethnic, homosexual-Kureishi), and cultural (cultural revolution and Maoism in China) issues, but they use rather traditional narrative techniques of social, and perhaps partly even of sentimental realism (Min). Although it cannot be said that these authors are untalented artists, they do not bring any significant formal, thematic and artistic innovations into the world literary context. Ethnic identity as well as inter-racial relationships have been treated much more interestingly and artistically in earlier works such as Joseph Contrad's *Heart of Darkness,* and, if we speak about the modern post-colonial context, in the works of John Coetzee, Peter Carey or Salman Rushdie, for example. Life under an authoritarian (communist) regime and its absurdities as depicted in Min's novel have been treated from various positions ranging from tragic to humorous in a multitude of works by Central and East European authors (e.g. Czech exile author Josef Škvorecký's novels, Milan Kundera's early novel *Joke* and many of his other novels and short stories). Thus these authors, Hanif Kureishi and Anchee Min, can be interesting from the culturological and sociological point of view as authors informing their audience either about the current state of inter-cultural, ethnic and sexual relationships or about the socio-historical and political condition in the past in a different country (Min). But notwithstanding the talent of these authors, they merely incorporate a relatively new theme into their old and traditional style and poetics. Early in the 20th century, trying to introduce a new poetics and the rhythms of the new period, the Imagists claimed that literature is not necessarily good when it speaks about new things using old language. As they argue,

"It is not good art to write badly about aeroplanes and automobiles; nor is it necessarily bad art to write well about the past"(Jones 1972:135).

Some of the above writers can be said to write "badly about aeroplanes", that is about a new theme, although the word "badly" might be too strong to describe these authors' indisputable talent.

In his novel, Hanif Kureishi uses the poetics of the traditional immigrant novel (ethnic, class issues) extended by a simplistic treatment of sexual issues (the homosexual relationship between a British and a Pakistani boy) evoking a metaphor of differentiated cultural (British-colonized) and sexual (heterosexual-homosexual) understanding. Using the autobiographical mode of the bildungsroman, Min depicts the emotional and physical suffering of a girl maturing during the cultural revolution in China, but her novel uses traditional poetics with predictable plot and characterization emphasizing a traditional struggle based on binary oppositions between good (anti-communism, anti-authoritarianism) and evil (communism, authoritarianism) as manifested in the narrator's perception of reality. On the other hand, the novels by other Asian-American authors such as Maxine Hong Kingston and Amy Tan give a much more convincing and aesthetically valuable picture of immigrant experience, ethnic identity, racial, class, and sexual (or "gender") relationships, cultural condition as well as "patriarchal oppression" by the use of an innovative poetics emphasizing the power of storytelling given from different perspectives (Amy Tan's *Joy Luck Club*), or by the incorporation of (Chinese) myths and "trickster" poetics (Gates, 1988; Smith, 1997) into their narratives.

Although a great number of books and studies has recently been published on the literature and culture of the USA, not so many scholarly books have been produced dealing with the role of aesthetics and ideology in American fiction and arts. Although similar to this book's approach, the book by Madelyn Jablon entitled *Black Metafiction: Self-Consciousness in African American Literature* (1999) has rather limited scope, as suggested by its closely-defined title. The essays included in the present book, however, give a broader, more interdisciplinary and comparative perspective on the subject, and deal with the working of aesthetics and ideology in American literature and arts as well as with the role of aesthetics and ideology in creating the imagery of American cultural identity (especially Obododimma Oha, who is the only exception and who does not deal primarily with the writing of an American author, but through analysis of William Blake's poetry he tries to identify the image of America as projected in the European mind). The book includes contributions by African, Central and West European, Asian and North American scholars investigating and comparing ideological and non-ideological approaches to the analysis of literary, artistic as well as popular works (popular music) mostly by American authors. Most of the papers (with the exception of John Stauffer's and Csaba Csapó's) were presented at the EAAS international conference on *The United States of/in Europe: Nationhood, Citizenship, Culture* held in Bordeaux, France, between March 22-25, 2002. They were presented in the Workshop 17 American Nation, Race, Gender, Class-Ideology of Art? which was chaired by the editor of this book. All contributions deal with the role of ideology and aesthetics in the creation of meaning in the texts discussed. Most of the essays deal with the way various aspects of American identity are depicted, represented, treated, ideologized and aestheticized in different literary genres, forms of art and media. The approach of most contributions varies from a certain defence of feminist and partly ideological positions and methods of analysis (Zoe Detsi-Diamanti, partly Pi-Hua Ni and Kallas) to closely mythical, semiotic, cultural and partly deconstructionist analyses of the artistic texts (other contributions). The publication of this book would not be possible without a fascinating technical help, formatting, creativity and patience of my colleague PaeDr. Ivana Cimermanová, PhD. from the Department of English Language and Literature, Faculty of Humanities and Natural Sciences, The University of Prešov, Slovakia.

Most of the contributions try to identify the valuable aspects of poetics and aesthetics of particular American authors and their role in the creation of both meaning and aesthetic experience. Although the emphasis of this book is on the role of the aesthetic or artistic quality of literary texts, space is also given to ideological positions and critical appreciations of ideology and politics rather than aesthetics (Detsi-Diamanti, Kallas). The contributions by the scholars included in this book offer multidisciplinary, cross-cultural and comparative perspectives and represent the diversity of scholarly voices ranging from general discussion on the relationship between ideology and art (Anton Pokrivčák), and between ideology and multiculturalism (Cristina Garrigós), through analysis of poetry (Pokrivčák, Obododima Oha), postmodern fiction (Pi-Hua Ni, Cristina Garrigós), and drama (Zoe Detsi-Diamanti, Csaba Csapó), to comparative analysis of the depiction of the identity of North American Indians in such different media as literature and film (Michal Peprník). In addition, the book includes analysis of Black rap music

(Wojciech Kallas). The chapters are arranged according to the genres and media discussed (analysis of the hybrid genre of autobiography and poetry in the first chapter is followed by analysis of postmodern fiction and (comparatively) film, and further by analysis of drama and music), arranged not necessarily, but mostly chronologically. I have decided to include Pepрník's comparative study of literary and film versions of the book in Chapter II dealing with postmodern fiction and film, since the author's analysis indicates a certain connection of the researched texts with postmodernism.

Part I deals with earlier genres such as autobiography, sociological, political and theoretical essays, but also with poetry and partly with theories. It includes a longer, more detailed paper by John Stauffer in which he analyzes mainly Frederick Douglass' novella *The Heroic Slave*, his speeches *My Bondage* and *My Freedom* as well as his works *Progress* (1861) and *Pictures* (1864), and suggests that Douglass was influenced by his reading of Aristotle's *Poetics* and *Politics* and possibly (as suggested by John Stauffer) by the idea of the sublime (I. Kant, E. Burke). Stauffer points out Douglass' attempt to find a connection between aesthetics and the social with the emphasis on the idea of liberty. In addition, he shows Douglass' search for an authentic black aesthetics. In his view, for Douglass, representations of slavery can evoke feelings of freedom and degrees of power. Stauffer emphasizes the way in which representations of freedom in Douglass' works create a crisis of language and aesthetics, and he explores these two forms of representation in Douglass's art.

In another paper, Obododima Oha explores the spiritualization and re/mythologizing of American history, especially in relation to the American confrontation with British imperialism. He shows that William Blake, an English author, reconstructs the history of America, turning American leaders and revolutionaries into mythical protagonists, and re-imagining the American context in ways that insert the exotic and the Gothic within a visualized empire of grandeur. Oha reads Blake's poem *America: A Prophecy* (1793) as a representation of a grand narrative in which America is understood as a continuation and complementation of Europe. In Oha's view then, in Blake's poem America is depicted and understood as a "New Europe" rather than a "New World."

In the same chapter, Anton Pokrivčák focuses on the representation of being in classical texts of American poetry such as those by Emily Dickinson and Wallace Stevens. In his essay, he emphasizes the aesthetic qualities of "ontological poetics" in the poetry of these authors, which he understands as poetics resisting ideological and political interpretations by dealing with the universal problem of being.

The subject of **Part II** is postmodern fiction and film. Cristina Garrigós' paper addresses four questions that are intended to open up a discussion on the problem of the connection between multiculturalism and postmodernism:

1. Multiculturalism's possible connection with the postmodern age and its character during this period;
2. Identity problems as part of the postmodern multicultural experience (on the one hand, minorities reaffirming their essential identity, and on the other hand, the postmodern questioning of this belief in its essence, proposing instead a constructed identity based on language);
3. Multiculturalism's possible denial of the Western Rationalistic Tradition (ethnic literatures' possible attempt to subvert the "master" historical Western discourse);
4. Contemporary ethnic narratives' connection to postmodernist (traditionally white and male) aesthetics.

In another paper in this chapter dealing with John Barth's fiction, Pi-Hua Ni analyzes the transition of Barth's fiction from an androcentric paradigm (in Barth's early fiction such as *The Floating Opera*, *The End of Road* and *Dunyazade*) to an androgynous one (Barth's later novel *Sabbatical: A Romance*). Ni has adapted feminist critique and the postmodern concept of gender-crossing first to analyze Barth's early patriarchal narrative paradigm and then to foreground the novelist's accomplishment in achieving an androgynous narrative. Ni also shows the way the postmodern poetics of John Barth's fiction is able to address ideological and social categories such as gender and class through an aesthetically and artistically valuable and convincing poetics as manifested in his novel *Sabbatical: A Romance.*

Michal Peprník's paper shows that Michael Mann's film adaptation of James Fenimore Cooper's novel of the same title, *The Last of the Mohicans* (1992), is an example of the latest, most radical and ideologically biased mutilation of the original text. In his view, the motif of revenge dominates this film. Focusing on the ideologization of the original narrative pattern of the pre-text (Cooper's novel) and its transformation in Mann's film version, Peprník argues that the film strongly legitimizes the violence of revenge as a pattern of justice-making behavior, and suppresses the option of forgiveness and reconciliation, a perspective associated with female characters in Cooper, and with the Quaker David Gamut in the novel.

The last part of this book, **Part III**, consists of papers dealing with forms of art other thanthe novel, that is drama, film and music.

In Zoe Detsi-Diamanti's view, nineteenth-century American drama strove to support the image of America as a free and democratic country of unlimited opportunities. This was, however, in contrast to the reality of everyday social and political life marked by growing racial inequality and oppression. In her paper, Detsi-Diamanti explores the way in which early American theatre consciously or unconsciously reflected the ambiguities of American society and rhetoric as it wavered between antithetical notions of reality/imagination, exclusion/inclusion, heterogeneity/ homogeneity, and repression/opportunity. The main emphasis is on the way nineteenth-century American drama both reinforced and undermined social structures, political functions and cultural symbols. She illustrates her points through analysis of early nineteenth century plays such as the popular social comedy by Anna Cora Mowatt *Fashion* (1845); George L. Aiken's *Uncle Tom's Cabin* (1852), and Dion Boucicault's *The Octoroon* (1859). Her emphasis is on analysis of the representations of Black-American protagonists and slavery as manifested in these plays.

In his paper, Csaba Csapó points out that certain literary texts, in this case David Mamet's play *Oleanna,* restrict or even resist interpretation when this is regarded only as study of the extent to which literary forms and conventions can be identified as (natural) manifestations of specific ideologemes or even as determining formats of particular ideological discourses. He emphasizes the aesthetic quality of the play which on the one hand shows the artistic mastery of the author, and deals on the other handwith currently highly-ideologized issues such as political correctness, sexual harassment and gender through the use of convincing and non-teleological poetics.

In his paper on African-American rap music, Wojciech Kallas analyses the lyrics of several songs by the well-known rap group *Public Enemy* and argues that their songs are what could be called "intellectual rap", since they make references to various events from the history of the black community in the USA. Kallas values *Public Enemy*'s rap because it seems to represent, in his view, much more than mere entertainment by serving an important social function. Kallas argues that rap songs, including these analyzed, reject the paternalistic ideology used by the federal government and promote the ideology of black racial superiority.

WORKS CITED

Belsey, K., Moore, J. (eds.) *The Feminist Reader: Essays in Gender and the Politics of Literary Criticism.* Basingstoke: Macmillan, 1989.

De Man, P."The Resistance to Theory."Yale French Studies 63 (1982):3-20.

Gates, H.L., Jr. *Figures in Black: Words, Signs, and the "Racial" Self.* New York: Oxford UP, 1987.

Gates, H.L., Jr. *The Signifying Monkey*. New York: Oxford UP, 1988.

Green, K., LeBihan, J. *Critical Theory&Practise: A Coursebook.* London and New York: Routledge, 1996.

Jablon, M. *Black Metafiction: Self-Consciousness in African American Literature.* Iowa City: University of Iowa Press, 1999.

Jones, P. (ed.). *Imagist Poetry*. London:Penguin, 1972.

Levin, R."The Cultural Materialist Attack on Artistic Unity and the Problem of Ideological Criticism." Harris, W.V. (ed.) *Beyond Poststructuralism. The Speculations of Theory and the Experience of Reading.* University Park:The Pennsylvania State University Press, 1996.137-156.

Newman, Ch. *The Postmodern Aura: The Act of Fiction in an Age of Inflation.* Evanston: Northwestern University Press, 1985.

Smith, J.R. *Writing Tricksters: Mythic Gambols in American Ethnic Literature.* Berkeley and London: University of California Press, 1997.

Weedon, C. *Feminist Practise and Post-Structuralist Theory*. Oxford: Blackwell, 1987.

Zavarzadeh, Mas'ud. "The Semiotics of the Foreseen: Modes of Narrative Intelligibility in (Contemporary) Fiction." *Poetics Today* 6: 4(1985): 607-626.

PART I

EARLY GENRES, POETRY AND THEORIES

I.1 John Stauffer: Frederick Douglass — Aesthetics, Ideology, and the Problem of Freedom

Long after he had escaped from bondage in 1838, Frederick Douglass insisted that he was still a slave. In 1844, while lecturing for the American Anti-Slavery Society, he emphasized that he was a fugitive "not *from* slavery", as advertisements for his lectures stated, but a fugitive "*in* slavery"— a fugitive and a slave.[1] And in 1849 he continued to refer to himself as a "fugitive slave", even though his legal freedom had been purchased by sympathizers in 1847.[2]

It is perhaps understandable that Douglass ends his 1845 *Narrative* not with freedom, but with feelings of bondage. At the end of the last chapter, just before the appendix, he describes his experience at anti-slavery meetings:

"I seldom had much to say at the meetings, because what I wanted to say was so much better said by others. But while attending an anti-slavery convention at Nantucket in 1841, I felt strongly moved to speak, and was at the same time much urged to do so. . . . It was a severe cross, and I took it up reluctantly. ***The truth was, I felt myself a slave****, and the idea of speaking to white people weighed me down"* [my emphasis]."[3]

Douglass's continued sense of bondage is a curious reversal from his famous fight with Edward Covey:

"This battle with Mr. Covey was the turning-point in my career as a slave",

he states in his *Narrative* (89).

---

[1] Nathaniel P. Rogers, "Southern Slavery and Northern Religion," Feb. 1, 1844, reprinted in David Blight, ed., *Narrative of the Life of Frederick Douglass, An American Slave* (Bedford/St. Martins, 2nd ed., 2003), p. 140.

[2] Douglass, "A Tribute for the Negro," in Philip Foner, ed., *The Life and Writings of Frederick Douglass*, vol. 1, p. 380.

[3] Blight, ed., *Narrative of the Life of Frederick Douglass*, p. 119 (emphasis added. Subsequent quotations from the *Narrative* are from this edition.

"It was a glorious resurrection, from the tomb of slavery, to the heaven of freedom. My long-crushed spirit rose, cowardice departed, bold defiance took its place; and I now resolved that, however long I might remain a slave in ***form****, the day had passed forever when I could be a slave in* ***fact*** [89, my emphasis]."

As a slave, Douglass felt free; as a free man, he felt himself a slave.

He resolves this paradox through art. At the Nantucket antislavery convention, he overcomes his feelings of bondage by performing for white people:

"I spoke but a few moments, when I felt a degree of freedom, and said what I desired with considerable ease"(119).

His fight with Covey is also a performance, a staged and ritualized battle through which he becomes "in fact" free (89). It is staged in the stables, and he brings Sandy's magical roots for protection. Douglass's description focuses primarily on controlling the fight's parameters. He wants it to be a "fair" contest between slave and master.[4] Bill Smith and William Hughes witness the fight, and Hughes threatens to interfere on Covey's behalf, but Douglass kicks him, "*fairly sicken[ing] him*", and he and Covey are left to fight their own battle (88).

"*We were at it for nearly two hours*", Douglass notes (88). Most of the fight is left to the reader's imagination, much as Douglass's performance at Nantucket is left to the reader's imagination. He stands up to whites rhetorically in the one instance, physically in the other. Both performances result in freedom. To paraphrase Douglass, representing the slave in form produces a free man in fact. But the performance itself is

[4] In *My Bondage and My Freedom* and in *Life and Times* (1892), Douglass states: "All was fair thus far." See Douglass, *My Bondage and My Freedom* ed. William L. Andrews (1855; reprint, Urbana: University of Illinois Press, 1987), p. 149; and Douglass, *Life and Times of Frederick Douglass, Written by Himself* (New York: Collier Books, 1962), p. 142. Subsequent quotations from *My Bondage and My Freedom* and *Life and Times* are from these edition.

only partially represented. The description is a synecdoche for the whole act.

Douglass believed that true art could break down social barriers. "True" art for him meant accurate and "authentic" representations of blacks, rather than caricatures such as blackface minstrelsy.[5] Through speeches, writings, and images, he created and refashioned a black public persona that became one of the most famous in the nineteenth century. In print, speech, and images he sought to fashion himself as an art object, or performer, that would confer upon both his persona and his white perceivers the "gift of life", to borrow from Elaine Scarry, which would link them together and dissolve social barriers.[6] The slave, a "thing", acquired life and humanity (in the minds of readers) when it was represented as an art object or performer. And the perceiver acquired new life by perceiving that thing as human. Freedom was a matter of aesthetics in both a rhetorical and representational sense: the slave acquired subjectivity by being represented; and the reader would, Douglass hoped, be transformed by this representation, leading to a new age of actual freedom. For Douglass, representations of slavery brought feelings of freedom and degrees of power. But representations of *freedom* created in him a crisis of language and aesthetics. I want to explore these two forms of representation in Douglass's art.

Throughout the 1850s and 1860s, Douglass pondered the relation of art to reform. He devoted two speeches to the subject, one called, *Pictures and Progress* (1861), and the other entitled *Pictures* (1864).[7]

---

[5] John Stauffer, *The Black Hearts of Men: Radical Abolitionists and the Transformation of Race* (Cambridge: Harvard University Press, 2002), esp. chapter two.

[6] Elaine Scarry, *On Beauty and Being Just* (Princeton: Princeton University Press, 1999), pp. 69, 90.

[7] Douglass, "Pictures and Progress," in John Blassingame, ed., *The Frederick Douglass Papers*, series 1, volume 3 (New Haven: Yale University Press, 1985), pp. 452-473; Douglass, "Pictures," holograph, n.d. [late 1864], Frederick Douglass Papers, Library of Congress. "Pictures" is a revised version of "Pictures and Progress"; it is a longer, more developed treatment of Douglass's understanding of aesthetics as it relates to politics. My quotations are from "Pictures."

Douglass defined "pictures" broadly to mean any form of representation. He felt that the picture-making process was a crucial aid to reform. In his mind all humans sought accurate representations both of "material reality" and of an "unseen spiritual world."[8] This affinity for pictures is what distinguished humans from animals. Douglass paraphrased the opening of Aristotle's *Poetics*, 3.1, by saying:

"Man is the only picture-making animal in the world. He alone of all the inhabitants of earth has the capacity for pictures."[9]

Emphasizing the humanity of all people was central to Douglass's reform vision, since all but the most radical of Americans defended inequality and racial hierarchies on the grounds that black slaves and their descendents were fundamentally different from other humans.

In a sense, Douglass embraced Aristotle's *Poetics* to attack Aristotle's *Politics*. In *Politics*, Aristotle articulated a natural slave ideal that would help shape virtually all subsequent proslavery thought.

"From the hour of their birth, some men are marked out for subjection, others for rule,"

Aristotle argued. He placed slaves on the same order as domesticated animals: an ox is "*the poor man's slave*," he famously said. Although ancient Greeks saw slavelike traits in "Barbarians," ancient slavery was not racialized in the way it came to be during the Atlantic slave trade. The absence of physical, or racialized, demarcations between slave and master bothered Aristotle. He recognized that some slaves

---

In *Black Hearts of Men*, I discuss these speeches in relation to Douglass's embrace of the visual image. He had his portrait taken at least as much as Whitman, who is legendary for visually creating and recreating himself. See Stauffer, *The Black Hearts of Men*, pp. 45-56; and my forthcoming essay on black abolition aesthetics and representations in Stauffer and Timothy McCarthy, *Millennial Vistas: New Essays on Abolitionism* (New York: The Free Press, 2004).

8 Douglass, "Pictures."

9 Douglass, "Pictures." In *Poetics* 3.1 Aristotle states: *"Imitation [or representation in other editions] comes naturally to human beings from childhood (and in this they differ from other animals, i.e. in having a strong propensity to imitation and in learning their earliest lessons through imitation)."* Aristotle, *Poetics* tr. and ed. Malcolm Heath (New York: Penguin Books, 1996), p. 6.

could have the bodies of free men, and that free men could become slaves through capture and sale. But these "injustices" did not alter Aristotle's conviction that people were by nature slaves or free, and he felt it was to their advantage and the good of society to maintain these distinctions. Unlike Douglass, Aristotle's belief in the "instinct for representation" did not pertain to slaves.[10]

Douglass attacked slavery and racism by championing the picture-making proclivity of all humans. In so doing he emphasized not only humanity's common origins, but the superiority of imagination over reason. The "*full identity of man with nature*," he said, "*is our chief distinction from all other beings on earth and the source of our greatest achievements.*" While "*dogs and elephants are said to possess*" the capacity for reason, only humans sought to recreate nature and portray both the "inside soul" and the "outside world" through such "artificial means" as pictures. Making pictures required imagination, and Douglass quoted Emerson to argue that the realm of the "imagination" was the "peculiar possession and glory of man." The power of the "imagination," he emphasized, was "*a sublime, prophetic, and all-creative power.*" It linked humans to *"the Eternal sources of life and creation,"* and allowed them to create and appreciate pictures as accurate representations of some greater reality. The power of the imagination helped people realize their sublime ideals in an imperfect world.[11]

The "sublime" power of the imagination could be used to create a performative self that would help usher in a new world of interracial equality. As Douglass aptly put it:

"Poets, prophets, and reformers are all picture makers— and this ability is the secret of their power and of their achievements. They see

---

[10] Aristotle, *The Politics*, tr. T.A. Sinclair (New York: Penguin Books, 1981), p. 67, 58; Thomas Wiedemann, *Greek and Roman Slavery* (London: Routledge, 1994), pp. 18-20 (I prefer Wiedemann's translation); David Brion Davis, *In the Image of God: Religion, Moral Values, and Our Heritage of Slavery* (New Haven: Yale University Press, 2001), pp. 128-129.
[11] Douglass, "Pictures."

what ought to be by the reflection of what is, and endeavor to remove the contradiction."[12]

He considered himself all three: a prophet, a poet (by which he meant "artist"), and reformer. As a prophet, he drew on divine sources to create sublime pictures of a new world. His aesthetic vision was sublime, darkly romantic, and apocalyptic. It embodied both the fulfillment of the nation's sacred ideals, and the desolation that would accompany this transformation. It was a millennial vision defined in nationalist terms.[13]

Douglass's use of the sublime is telling, for it was his preferred form to represent slavery and seek a transformation from the slave as thing into a human who was equal in humanity to the perceiver. Although it is unclear whether or not Douglass had read Edmund Burke or Immanuel Kant on the sublime, he knew of Burke and referred to him in an 1851 speech, and his understanding of the sublime closely approximates that of Burke.[14] The sublime inspired empathic understanding; it narrowed the distance between spectator and actor. It was a mode of persuasion that drew on the spiritual and emotional qualities of a work of art. It sought to

---

[12] Douglass, "Pictures."

[13] See Stauffer, *The Black Hearts of Men*, esp. chapter one. On the sublime, I have relied on the following sources: Edmund Burke, *A Philosophical Enquiry into the Origin of Our Ideas of the Sublime and Beautiful*, ed. J.T. Boulton (1958; reprint, Notre Dame: University of Notre Dame Press, 1968); Immanuel Kant, *Observations on the Feeling of the Beautiful and Sublime*, tr. John T. Goldthwait (Berkeley: University of California Press, 1960); Kant, *Critique of the Power of Judgment*, tr. Paul Guyer and Eric Matthews (Cambridge: Cambridge University Press, 2000), pp. 89-159; Thomas Weiskel, *The Romantic Sublime: Studies in the Structure and Psychology of Transcendence* (Baltimore: Johns Hopkins University Press, 1976), esp. pp. 3-23; Elaine Scarry, *On Beauty*, pp. 81-86; Philip Fisher, *Wonder, the Rainbow, and the Aesthetics of Rare Experience* (Cambridge: Harvard University Press, 1998), pp. 1-32; Steven Knapp, *Personification and the Sublime: Milton to Coleridge* (Cambridge: Harvard University Press, 1985); Bryan J. Wolf, *Romantic Re-Vision: Culture and Consciousness in Nineteenth-Century American Painting and Literature* (Chicago: University of Chicago Press, 1982), esp. ch. 5; and Richard Klein, *Cigarettes Are Sublime* (Durham: Duke University Press, 1993).

[14] Douglass lauds Burke for his eloquence in championing Catholic emancipation. See Douglass, "Persecution on Account of Faith, Persecution on Account of Color: An Address . . . on 26 January 1851," Blassingame, ed., *Frederick Douglass Papers*, series 1, volume 2 (New Haven: Yale University Press, 1982), pp. 293-294.

persuade the viewer to see the world in a different light. Burke emphasized that sublimity evoked delightful horror or terrible joy. Terror, as Burke stressed,

"is a passion which always produces delight when it does not press too close, and pity is a passion accompanied with pleasure, because it arises from love and social affection."

For Burke, God had endowed people with a capacity for delighting in the pain of others, and it was this very pleasure that made benevolence possible:

"if this passion was simply painful, we would shun with the greatest care all persons and places that could excite such a passion."

There was also a racial dimension to sublimity; for Burke and Douglass both, blackness was a prime source of the sublime. Blackness evoked both the pain and terror as well as the delight and joy that was central to the meaning of the sublime. Douglass's sublime aesthetic was a black aesthetic. But unlike Burke, he sought to realize it, rather than take comfort in the fact, as Burke did, that the sublime was only a representation, which kept the reality of pain and terror at a safe distance.[15]

---

[15] Edmund Burke, *A Philosophical Enquiry into the Origin of Our Ideas of the Sublime and Beautiful*, pp. xlv, lvi-lvii, 39, 46 (quoted), 51, 58-59, 143-149; Douglass, "Pictures"; David Brion Davis, *The Problem of Slavery in Western Culture* (New York: Oxford University Press, 1966), 358, 448.

Burke treats both blackness and darkness as aspects of the sublime; they differed in that blackness was a more confined idea, referring especially to color and "*coloured bodies*" (147). Blackness and darkness were sublime because they led to obscurity, and *"to make any thing terrible, obscurity seems in general to be necessary. When we know the full extent of any danger, when we accustom our eyes to it, a great deal of the apprehension vanishes*"(58-59). Moreover, blackness caused pain because it contracted the *"radial fibres of the iris"* so as to *"strain the nerves that compose it beyond their natural tone; and by this means to produce a painful sensation"* (145-146). For Douglass, blackness was sublime because of the terror by which whites treated blacks.

The distinction between Burke's and Douglass's understanding of the sublime resembles that between Enlightenment and Romantic thinkers. Douglass and other Romantic radicals embraced their sublime vision, seeking to realize it. In confronting the terror and exhilaration of the sublime, Douglass hoped that the viewer would

Douglass went so far as to suggest that the *"moral and social influence of pictures"*—and *"representation"* more generally— were more important in shaping the nation than "*the making of its laws.*"[16] Art, and particularly sublime art, was more important than politics for changing society. It is a remarkable statement, for Douglass always defined himself as an abolitionist and reformer, and throughout the 1850s and 1860s he was deeply committed to political action. But art was the engine of social change.

The Heroic Slave, Douglass's only work of fiction and the first African-American novella, highlights the power that a sublime vision— in the form of a black slave— can have over a white subject. Published in 1853, the story is a fictionalized account of the historical Madison Washington, a Virginia slave who escaped to Canada, returned to free his wife, was reenslaved in the attempt, and sent South to New Orleans on the slave ship *Creole*, where he led a successful mutiny. Aside from these facts, Douglass new almost nothing about the historical Madison Washington. By representing him in fiction, he sought to transform him into art, thus giving him life and furthering the cause of freedom.

The novella opens with Mr. Listwell, a white man, chancing upon Madison Washington, who is talking to himself in the forest and vowing to be free. Washington is characterized in sublime terms that evoke both terror and joy: he is *"black but comely"* (a paraphrase of Song of Solomon, 1:5); his eye is *"lit with emotion,"* and keeps *"guard under a brow as dark and as glossy as the raven's wing"*; and his voice *"could terrify as well as charm." "His whole appearance betokened Herculean strength; yet there was nothing savage or forbidding in his aspect."* He

---

encounter a moment of psychological reversal: an oppressive burden would be lifted, and the soul would receive an influx of power and experience an ecstasy of liberation and release. See Bryan Jay Wolf, *Romantic Re-Vision*, p. 177; Thomas Weiskel, *The Romantic Sublime*, pp. 83-106; Stauffer, *Black Hearts of Men*, pp. 27-28, 33-35.

[16] Douglass, „Pictures and Progress," in Blassingame, *Frederick Douglass Papers*, 1:3, p. 456.

has "*a giant's strength, but not a giant's heart.*" He is "*one to be sought as a friend, but to be dreaded as an enemy.*" And in his desire to be free, he identifies with the wild beasts of the forest: the "*accursed and crawling snake*," and the "*raging bull.*" Douglass transposes Washington's "*savage and forbidding aspects,*" which were terms used by racists to justify black oppression, into the sublime (38-39).[17]

Mr. Listwell is transformed by Washington's sublimity. During Washington's "soliloquy," he stands at the edge of the forest, and gazes at Washington without the latter's knowledge.[18] He feels guilty for intruding, but has "*long desired to sound the mysterious depths of the thoughts and feelings of a slave*" (40). Immediately after witnessing Washington's performance, Listwell becomes a new man. The sight and sound of Washington rang "*through the chambers of*" Listwell's "*soul, and vibrated through his entire frame*"(41). He realizes that the slave is not a "*thing*" but a "*man,*" "*a child of God,--guilty of no crime but the color of his skin, hiding away from the face of humanity*"(41). He is converted to Washington's cause: "*From this hour,*" he vows,

"*I am an abolitionist. I have seen and heard enough, and shall go home resolved to atone for my past indifference to this ill-starred race*"(42).

---

[17] Douglass's description of Madison Washington is also grotesque, bordering on kitsch. But the grotesque and kitsch also relate to the sublime. As Philip Fisher has noted, "*the sublime was an aesthetic category more important in the realm of kitsch than in high art. . . . It has more in common with such effects as the noble, the pious, or the grotesque, that area of the aesthetics where we most often find second-rate artists compensating by invoking either strong effects or right thinking.*" See Fisher, *Wonder, The Rainbow, and the Aesthetics of Rare Experience*, p. 2. On the sublime as a category of the grotesque, see William Van O'Connor, *The Grotesque: An American Genre and Other Essays* (Carbondale: Southern Illinois University Press, 1962), p. 5.

[18] Douglass, *The Heroic Slave*, in Ronald T. Takaki, ed., *Violence in the Black Imagination: Essays and Documents, Expanded Edition* (New York: Oxford University Press, 1993), p. 38. Subsequent quotations from *Heroic Slave* are from this edition.

Listwell is aptly named: as someone who has the capacity to "listen well," he is Douglass's vision of an ideal white man.[19] He is an astute observer of blacks: by perceiving them, he learns to treat them as humans and equals.

When the two men meet again, five years have elapsed, but Listwell immediately recognizes Washington: *"From that hour, your face seemed to be daguerreotyped on my memory"*(45). "Daguerreotyping" a character was a common trope in abolitionist narration; Harriet Beecher Stowe, for instance, "daguerreotype[s]" Uncle Tom "for our readers."[20] It conveyed more than physical description or even photographic memory, for a daguerreotype was thought to penetrate the perceiver's soul as well as his mind. Daguerreotypes were frequently described in sublime terms. For Holgrave, the fictional daguerreotypist from Hawthorne's *House of Seven Gables*, there was something both delightful and terrible about his art. *"There is a wonderful insight in heaven's broad and simple sunshine,"* Holgrave says of the daguerreotype. At the same time, it

"brings out the secret character with a truth that no painter would ever venture upon, even could he detect it. There is, at least, no flattery in my humble line of art" (Hawthorne 1961: 85).

Nadar, the famous French daguerreotypist who is best-known for his portraits of artists, specifically invoked the "sublime" in his characterization of daguerreotypy.[21]

Americans in particular saw God's work in the daguerreotype. Douglass and his contemporaries in the 1850s widely believed that daguerreotypes were "likenesses" in a religious sense— part of the

---

[19] See Robert Stepto, "Storytelling in Early Afro-American Fiction: Frederick Douglass's 'The Heroic Slave,'" *Georgia Review* 36 (1982): 355-368.

[20] Harriet Beecher Stowe, *Uncle Tom's Cabin; or, Life Among the Lowly* (New York: Penguin Books, 1981), p. 68.

[21] Nathaniel Hawthorne, *The House of Seven Gables* (New York: The New American Library, 1961), p. 85; Nadar, "Balzac and the Daguerreotype," *Literature and Photography: Interactions, 1840-1990*, ed. Jane M. Rabb (Albuquerque: University of New Mexico Press, 1995), p. 7. See also Richard Rudisill, quoted in Vicki Goldberg,ed., *Photography in Print: Writings from 1816 to the Present* (Albuquerque: University of New Mexico Press, 1981), pp. 74-76.

individual's essence, "a matter of spiritual similarity" rather than a mere "picture", according to W.J.T. Mitchell.[22] A daguerreotype, it was thought, contained part of the body and soul of the subject. Unlike subsequent forms of photography, daguerreotypes were unique objects, rather than a negative-to-positive process that allowed infinite reproductions. Having Washington daguerreotyped on Listwell's memory connects the two men's souls, and they become equals and friends. Both men benefit from their friendship: Listwell gains his spiritual freedom by atoning for his sin of indifference to slavery; and Washington gains his physical freedom, with help from his friend. But like Douglass's *Narrative*, the novella ends at the moment of Washington's freedom.

When Douglass published *My Bondage and My Freedom* in 1855, he was a political abolitionist, a temperate revolutionary, and an independent editor and intellectual. He had abandoned the paternalistic influence of William Lloyd Garrison, and had severed his ties to the American Anti-Slavery Society, which was committed to nonviolence and considered politics and government to be corrupt. He joined the National Liberty party, altered his newspaper to reflect his political views, and a few months before publishing *My Bondage*, became a founding member of the Radical Abolition party and attended its inaugural convention. In Radical Abolitionists he found white allies he could trust: he became close friend with Gerrit Smith and John Brown, who were also founding members of the party. Smith helped fund his newspaper, and Brown encouraged his endorsement of militancy. Both men treated him as an equal rather than as a son or dependent, as Garrison did.[23]

The Radical Abolition party was one of the most radical to date in America. Members embraced immediate abolition, full suffrage for all Americans regardless of sex or skin color; the redistribution of land so that no one would be rich and no one poor; and violent intervention against the growing belligerence of the Slave Power. And they relied on

---

[22] W.J.T. Mitchell, *Iconology: Image, Text, Ideology* (Chicago: University of Chicago Press, 1986), p. 31.
[23] See Stauffer, *The Black Hearts of Men*, chapters one and five.

"*pentecostal visitations*"(messages from God) to pave the way to a new world.[24] The black physician James McCune Smith, who wrote the Introduction to *My Bondage*, chaired the party's inaugural convention (The next time a black man chaired a national political convention was in 1988, when Ron Brown chaired the Democratic National Convention).[25] Political action offered Douglass a way to maintain a dynamic balance between his vision of a new world and the sinful present. The Radical Abolition party was in one sense a manifestation of members' sublime aesthetic. Most other reformers confined the sublime to the realm of art, which kept the reality of pain and terror at a safe distance. In seeking to realize their sublime vision, Douglass and his comrades experienced an ecstasy of liberation and release, as though the oppressive burden of sin and its attendant hierarchies had been lifted at last.[26]

From the first pages of *My Bondage*, Douglass represents himself as a confident black intellectual who borrows from white literary culture and scripture to shape his black aesthetic. *My Bondage* contains quotations or paraphrases from Coleridge, Sir Walter Scott, Shakespeare, Lord Byron, Aristotle, Milton, Martin Luther, William Cowper, Longfellow, Whittier, and there are least 35 separate biblical references. These references reveal not only Douglass's growing intellectual powers; they highlight his efforts to break down the color line. He anticipates W.E.B. Du Bois' famous maxim from *The Souls of Black Folk*: *"I sit with Shakespeare and he winces not."* Like Du Bois, the Douglass of *My Bondage* seeks to become a "*co-worker in the kingdom of culture*", dwell above the veil of race, and merge his double self— a black man and an American— "into a better and truer self."[27]

---

[24] *Proceedings of the Convention of Radical Political Abolitionists, Held At Syracuse, New York, June 26th, 27th, and 28th, 1855* (New-York: Central Abolition Board, 1855), p. 45. See also *Black Hearts of Men*, p. 12.

[25] Peter J. Boyer, "Ron Brown's Secrets," *The New Yorker*, June 9, 1997, p. 67. Boyer mistakenly says that Ron Brown was the first black to chair a national political convention.

[26] Stauffer, *The Black Hearts of Men*, chapters one and four.

[27] Du Bois, *The Souls of Black Folk* (New York: Penguin Books, 1989), pp. 90, 5.

The epigraph from Coleridge on the title page of *My Bondage* conveys something of Douglass's design:

"By a principle essential to Christianity, a PERSON is eternally differenced from a THING; so that the idea of a HUMAN BEING, necessarily excludes the idea of PROPERTY IN THAT BEING."[28]

Divine law, which Douglass viewed as co-extensive with natural and civil law, prohibited slavery. A person could not be a thing. The source of the quotation is itself significant: it is a slight revision of a line from Coleridge's *Preliminary Treatise on Method*, which served as the introductory essay of *Encyclopaedia Metropolitana* (1818), and was later revised for *The Friend.*[29] Coleridge's *Treatise* developed a method for a compendium of human knowledge. That Douglass read it suggests that he was interested in creating his own encyclopedia— or that *My Bondage and My Freedom* represented an encyclopedia of Douglass's life to date.

In the opening pages of *My Bondage*, Douglass reveals his revolutionary ethos. The frontispiece depicts him elegantly dressed but with his hands clenched in fists as though ready for a fight. It sends a message that is repeated throughout the book— one of artful defiance, or "majestic in his wrath," to quote one admirer.[30] The frontispiece illustrates, as it were, Douglass's sublime and black aesthetic: there is an incongruity between his black body and his white hands; between the rich details of his body and the rough sketch of his fists; between the majestic orator and someone who rejects words for blows. The image is meant to evoke both terror and delight.

Following the frontispiece is his elaborate dedication to Gerrit Smith (see Figure 2), who became for Douglass what Listwell was for Madison

---

[28] Douglass, *My Bondage and My Freedom*, p. 1.

[29] H. J. Jackson and J.R. de J. Jackson, eds., *The Collected Works of Samuel Taylor Coleridge, vol. 11: Shorter Works and Fragments, vol. 1* (Princeton: Princeton University Press, 1995), pp. 671, 628.

[30] Elizabeth Cady Stanton, quoted in Frederick S. Voss, *Majestic in His Wrath: A Pictorial Life of Frederick Douglass* (Washington, D.C.: Smithsonian Institution Press, 1995), p. v.

Washington— a good listener, a spiritual friend, and an effective promoter, prompter, and agent of Douglass's black persona. Gerrit Smith and Madison Washington are the only two historical characters in *The Heroic Slave*; and while Listwell resembles Douglass's perception of Gerrit Smith, Madison Washington suggests something of Douglass's own self-conception. In his dedication Douglass praises Smith for *"ranking slavery with piracy and murder" and denying its legal and constitutional existence"* (2).

There is sublimity in the dedication as well. Like the frontispiece, it evokes both terror and delight— the terror of violence with the delight of friendship— and friendship was itself a characteristic of the sublime, according to Kant.[31] The elaborate script threatens to overwhelm the words, suggesting that Douglass wants his words to be seen and felt as much as read and heard. He wants the perceiver to feel the texture of these words, and to be transformed by them. The dedication is also grotesque, a category in which the sublime typically appears, in seeking to fuse two incompatible realms: it blurs Douglass as the subject with Gerrit Smith as the object of Douglass's dedication. Both men are on together on the page. At the outset of *My Bondage*, then, Douglass declares that slavery represents a state of rebellion or war, which needs to be vanquished with physical force if necessary in order to preserve the peace.

McCune Smith's Introduction to *My Bondage* focuses almost exclusively on Douglass's accomplishments as a free man and stresses his importance as a "*Representative American man*" (17). The "secret" of Douglass's performative power, McCune Smith argues, stems from his success in continually transforming himself: he has

"passed through every gradation of rank comprised in our national make-up, and bears upon his persona and upon his soul every thing that is American" (17).

[31] Kant, *Observations on the Feeling of the Beautiful and Sublime*, p. 52.

For McCune Smith, Douglass is a symbol of America, his progress made "visible" by his remarkable "style" of writing and speaking (20). McCune Smith draws attention to Douglass's mixed blood, and emphasizes that

"for his energy, perseverance, eloquence, [. . .] and wide sympathy, he is indebted to his negro blood" (22).

The Representative American man, like America itself, was a mixture of races. Near the end of the Introduction, he argues that the Egyptians— the originators of western culture— like the Americans, *"were a mixed race, with some negro blood circling around the throne"* (23).

While McCune Smith focuses on Douglass as a free man, Douglass represents himself as a slave who acquires life through performance (becoming art), and then triumphs over whites. In his fight with Covey, which is now witnessed by three people instead two, Douglass emphasizes even more than in the *Narrative* his controlled performance, and his victory: Covey *"had been mastered by a boy of sixteen,"* he notes (152). It is also a sublime performance: It is the turning point in his life as a slave, but it is also *"undignified,"* for *"the fighting madness had come upon"* him (151, 149). And there are "comic" elements to it, as when Bill, who knows that Covey wants him to help, feigns ignorance and pretends not to know what to do (150). *"I had reached the point, at which I was* ***not afraid to die****"*, he concludes (152). By courting the horrors of death, Douglass experiences the ecstasy of freedom.

Douglass appropriately ends the chapter with a quote from Lord Byron's *Childe Harold's Pilgrimage*:

"Hereditary bondmen, know ye not / Who would be free, themselves must strike the blow?" (153).

The line became a common refrain for Douglass and his comrades in the 1850s—McCune Smith quotes the same line in *the Introduction.* Byron seemed to embody in both his life and poetry Douglass's ideal of the Representative American: a male liberator and freedom fighter who dispensed with fixed markers of social status and sought continual self-transformation while remaining *"constant,"* as Byron put it, in his *"strong love of liberty."*[32]

My Bondage and My Freedom is divided into two parts—"life as a slave" and "life as a free man." While Douglass creates a powerful black persona during his life in slavery, the second part gives him considerable trouble. He had never before represented himself as a free man, and it provoked a crisis of aesthetics. He begins this section by saying:

"There is no necessity for any extended notice of the incidents of this part of my life" (205). His description of becoming free a few lines later reveals a similar frustration with the inadequacy of words:

"It was a moment of joyous excitement, which no words can describe. . . . In a letter to a friend, written soon after reaching New York, I said I felt as one might be supposed to feel, on escaping from a den of hungry lions. But, in a moment like that, sensations are too intense and rapid for words" (205).

The power of words, acquired in part by reading and rereading *The Columbian Orator*, had first fueled Douglass's desire for freedom and enabled his rise to fame. But now words could not represent the sensation of freedom.

From one perspective, the problem arose because Douglass had no one to turn to for help. In the genre of slave narratives, there was no precedent for representing oneself as a freeman while also envisioning immediate emancipation. Slave narrators focused on their life in bondage and described the horrors of slavery in the hope of converting readers to abolitionism. The teleology of slave narratives centered around the moment of freedom. But narratives of freedom had not been developed. Narrators saw in one divine event the end of doubt and disappointment; freedom represented a new age, and they worshipped it with unwavering faith. Traditional narrative forms could not describe this new dispensation. The struggle to find an aesthetics of freedom perhaps helps to explain why African-American literary works published in the 1850s greatly

---

[32] Anne Barton, "Not an Ideal Husband," *The New York Review of Books*, November 18, 1999, p. 46; Stauffer, *The Black Hearts of Men*, pp. 60-62, 85, 113, 150-151.

exceeds the works published between 1867 and 1876, a period of legal freedom in which only two novels were published and slave narratives dwindled to a trickle.[33]

In light of Douglass's hesitation about representing himself as a freeman, he devotes seventy pages to his *life as a freeman*, plus an additional sixty pages of an *Appendix* in small print that contains excerpts of six speeches and one public letter. That's a lot of prose to describe something he suggests cannot be described with words. He resolves the conundrum by emphasizing his subaltern status and his continued struggle for freedom in the face of northern racism and the paternalism of Garrisonians. He notes that after entering the ranks of the Garrisonian lecture circuit, he was treated as a commodity, or text, of white abolitionists, rather than having the autonomy to represent himself:

"I was generally introduced as a 'chattel'— a 'thing'— a piece of southern 'property'—the chairman assuring the audience that it could speak[...] 'Give us the facts,' said Collins, 'we will take care of the philosophy.'[...]But it was impossible for me to repeat the same old story month after month, and to keep up my interest in it[...][T]o go through with it every night was a task altogether too mechanical for my nature. 'Tell your story, Frederick,' would whisper my then revered friend, William Lloyd Garrison. I could not always obey, for I was now reading and thinking"(220).

The slave as "thing" could not become art and human because Garrisonians sought to control Douglass's creative self-fashioning. It was another form of bondage. Douglass's attack of Garrison is subtle but sharp: his *then* revered friend made him feel like a mechanical thing; he yearned for liberation, and could not always obey.[34]

---

[33] Henry Louis Gates, Jr., "The Trope of a New Negro and the Reconstruction of the Image of the Black," *The New American Studies: Essays from Representations*, ed. Philip Fisher (Berkeley: University of California Press, 1991), p. 321.

[34] I am grateful to William E. Cain's analysis for help developing my argument. See Cain, ed., *William Lloyd Garrison and the Fight Against Slavery: Selections for The Liberator* (Boston: Bedford Books, 1995), p. 48.

It is significant that Douglass ends his *life as a freeman* at the moment he severs ties with Garrison. He ends the narrative proper much as he does in his 1845 *Narrative*— at the moment of freedom. But in *My Bondage*, that moment represents his cultural declaration of independence from white paternalism. Then begins his Appendix, and Douglass radically alters his narrative framework. In struggling to create a new genre and to find an appropriate style for representing himself as a freeman, Douglass presents himself as an art object, a performer unadorned, as it were— unmediated by a narrator. He arranges the speeches chronologically, so that readers can glimpse the evolution of this public persona, ending in early 1855, with a speech on the antislavery movement that prophesies the new age.

In one sense, the narrative structure suggested by the speeches is sublime: it is a view of Douglass's recent past that is fragmented, not orderly, and inexplicable from the perspective that no narrator seeks to explain the subject. The speeches encourage readers to ascertain Douglass as a free persona, but in a boundless state, exceeding limits. These are the characteristics of sublime histories first sketched out by Friedrich von Schiller and most recently by Hans Kellner. As Kellner notes, *"as the sublime became a dominant aesthetic principle of Romantic art in general"* historical writing became "desublimated", and turned to "*beautification to fill the logically designated slot in the order of words as the antiliterature*"—a focus on "*the real as against the possible",* on rational, dispassionate, "*master narratives.*" *My Bondage and My Freedom* is, among other things, a history of the self, and in the Appendix its history of the free self is sublime, evoking what is possible rather than denoting what actually happened.[35]

---

[35] Hans Kellner, "However Imperceptibly: From the Historical to the Sublime," *PMLA* 118:3 (May 2003): 591-596, quotation from p. 592. See also Friedrich von Schiller, "On the Sublime," *"Naive and Sentimental Poetry" and "On the Sublime": Two Essays*, tr. J.A. Elias (New York: Ungar, 1966). One might say that while Douglass's *representation* of himself as a slave is sublime, his *history* of himself as a free man is sublime.

Many readers of *My Bondage* skim through or even skip the *Appendix* (it is never discussed). But it contains some of Douglass's most powerful writings, including *What to the Slave is the Fourth of July* and *The Slavery Party*, the latter of which anticipates, in its description of the Slave Power and its rhetorical power, Lincoln's famous *House Divided* speech of 1858. The speeches are well chosen and edited, and imply a continuation of Douglass's persona. But the focus is now on politics and nation. The performative slave has become political persona. The first speech is from Douglass's trip to England in 1846, which led directly to his legal freedom. In other speeches, he attacks his former master, Thomas Auld; connects his personal story to the nation's repudiation of its revolutionary ideals; and describes the Slave Power's attempt to

"padlock the lips of whites in order to secure the fetters on the limbs of the blacks" (Douglass 297).

Taken together, the speeches contrast the present sinful society with the vision of millennium; and the fragmented form complements the millennial history that Douglass envisions. With slavery and racism on the rise, Douglass had to envision a sharp break from the past in order to believe in an impending new age of freedom. A linear, rational vision of progress, and an unbroken orderly narrative, did not fit his existing circumstances and thus did not make sense to him.

That Douglass ended *My Bondage* with speeches was appropriate for another reason: he considered public speaking to be the most effective abolitionist tool and his greatest accomplishment as an artist and activist. *"I hardly need say to those who know me"*, he wrote near the end of his life, *"that writing for the public eye never came quite as easily to me as speaking to the public ear."* [36]

His oratory was the envy of public men of all persuasions. A well-known Whig editor and politician, (and no friend of black abolitionists), after hearing Douglass speak in early 1855, told a white friend:

---

[36] Douglass, *Life and Times*, p. 511.

"I would give twenty thousand dollars if I could deliver that address in that manner" (21). (It would be like saying today: *"I would give a million bucks if I could give a speech like that."*)

Douglass considered a speech to be a more authentic and immediate form of self-representation than writing. More than the pen, a speech could evoke the sublime: it appealed to the imagination more than to reason; and had a more powerful effect on the senses than words on a page. The pen could be powerful, but proslavery advocates used the pen *"with considerable impunity"*, as Douglass noted: *"ink and paper have no sense of shame."*[37] But slaveowners seldom ventured into abolitionist meetings, and were afraid of their speeches.A speech, like a daguerreotype, could more easily penetrate the soul. As Douglass became more learned, so too did his speeches. In the 1850s he began regularly to write out his speeches, toured the Lyceum circuit, and gradually abandoned his brilliant use of mimicry— which drew howls of laughter— for he increasingly felt it inappropriate to his subject.

Yet even in speeches Douglass had difficulty representing freedom. One such crisis occurred in response to the coming Jubilee. At a meeting at the A.M.E. Zion Church at Rochester, New York, on December 28, 1862, four days *before the Emancipation Proclamation* went into effect, he began a speech by saying: *"This is scarcely a day for prose. It is a day for poetry and song, a new song.'*[38] Here was one of the most famous public speakers in America, beginning a speech by saying it was no time for speeches. A speech could not convey the message and emotions he wanted to convey. The genre was inappropriate to the moment. He had lost faith in the aesthetics of his argument.

But then he gave a brilliant speech. It was one of his shortest speeches — about ten minutes in length, as opposed to his usual two-hour performances. And it focused on the meaning of the impending

---

[37] Douglass, "From the Editor," *The North Star*, November 23, 1849.

[38] Douglass, "The Day of Jubilee Comes," Blassingame, ed., *The Frederick Douglass Papers*, 1:3, p. 543.

Emancipation Proclamation and the continued duties of the lovers of liberty. He warned his audience that

"slavery has existed in this country too long and has stamped its character too deeply and indelibly, to be blotted out in a day or a year, or even in a generation. The slave will yet remain in some sense a slave, long after the chains are taken from his limbs, and the master will retain much of the pride, arrogance, imperiousness, conscious superiority, and love of power, acquired by his former position of master."

Although the slave will cease being *"the abject slave of a single master, his enemies will endeavor to make him the slave of society at large."*[39]

As a result, friends of freedom would still be needed, and an abolitionist speech would still be needed. In one sense, Douglass's form of representation corresponded with his message. A new age of legal freedom was at hand. Given his apocalyptic thinking— he likened the war to *Revelations* 12, where Michael and his angels battled against Satan— it is understandable that he had doubts about prose being the appropriate form to describe the dawn of a new age. An eschatological leap, a sharp break in linear chronology, could not effectively be conveyed in prose (except as he had attempted in *the Appendix* of *My Bondage*). Hence, the shortness of his speech. But at the same time, people would seek to preserve the existing social order, and continue to define society around binary conceptions of freedom and slavery, black and white. Slavery in some form would continue; and so it remained a day for prose.

By the time Douglass published the first edition of *Life and Times* (1881), his third autobiography, he had been out of slavery for forty-three years and legally free for thirty-four years. Since publishing *My Bondage and My Freedom*, he had departed considerably from his revolutionary ethos, and was more of an insider than ever before. He had been a White House guest of Lincoln three times; served as President of the insolvent Freedman's Bank; and in 1876, when Republicans abandoned the project

[39] Douglass, "Day of Jubilee," p. 545.

of Reconstruction by removing federal troops from the South, he was appointed marshal of the District of Columbia by President-Elect Rutherford B. Hayes. His appointment masked the concessions Republicans made to white supremacists to get Hayes elected. He had become a "Republican Wheelhorse" in the felicitous phrase of Benjamin Quarles.[40]

Life and Times recounts Douglass's achievements and betrays his retreat from his former pluralist vision. The book is a reminiscence— a desublimated history— and its principal object is not so much to change society, but to remind readers that the story of slavery should not be forgotten. Even in this it failed, for unlike his first two autobiographies, which were bestsellers, *Life and Times* sold few copies. It reads as Romantic history— the biography of a self and its times. With legal freedom, Douglass abandoned his sublime aesthetic; and his history is now linear, rational, dispassionate, and secular rather than millennial and grotesque. In a small way, he participates in the reconciliation between North and South by downplaying race. In *My Bondage* he embraces a sublime black self; in *Life and Times*, his desublimated self has become much whiter.

In *Life and Times*, Douglass flattens out his climactic fight with Covey. It is no longer the prominent and memorable scene it was in the earlier two narratives. While the language of the fight is similar to that of *My Bondage and My Freedom*, he has taken the emotion out of it. Gone are the exclamation marks, the capitalized words, and almost all of the italicized phrases, which he had used effectively in the earlier telling to evoke passion beyond what words alone could convey. He no longer seeks to evoke a sense of terror and delight, but rather to tell a dispassionate story. It is an imitation of an earlier scene and self, and lacks the power and originality of the earlier description. The fighting slave now seems simply "mad" rather than a sublime performer (140). And the

---

[40] Benjamin Quarles, *Frederick Douglass* (1948; reprint, New York: Da Capo Press, 1997), chapter fourteen.

means of achieving freedom, like the fight itself, is "undignified" rather than grotesque (143).

Throughout *Life and Times* Douglass whitewashes racial tensions. His tone is one of forgiveness rather than majestic wrath. There is little mention of his quarrel with Garrison. *"My **then** revered friend, Mr. Garrison*" now becomes simply *"my revered friend"* (217). In fact he reconciles almost all of his former tensions with Garrisonians by saying: *"To these friends,[...] I owe my success in life"*(467). He also seeks to reconcile North and South, master and slave. He reunites with his former master, Thomas Auld. Now, Douglass "loves" him, saying: "I did not run away from *you*, but from *slavery*"(443). It is an astonishing statement that ignores Auld's culpability for the crime of slavery. And it is a far cry from the militancy of *My Bondage*, where Douglass states: if a slave

"kills his master, he imitates only the heroes of the revolution. Slaveholders I hold to be individually and collectively responsible for all the evils"

of slavery (119). While Douglass forgives his former master in *Life and Times*, he castigates *"the rank and file"* of blacks: *"They,"* not whites, *"are among the first to deny and denounce*" the *"doctrine of human equality,"* he argues (411).

In *Life and Times*, Douglass also accepts beliefs in innate differences between blacks and whites, which he had vigorously repudiated during the 1850s. The longest excerpt in *Life and Times* is an 1879 speech on the recent exodus of blacks from the South. He opposes northern migration partly because he thinks blacks are "naturally" suited to warmer climates, and can thus better compete with whites in the South: "*Nature itself comes to the rescue of the Negro"* in the South, he writes. Whites cannot labor in the hot sun, and instead *"seek the shade of the verandas."* The Negro, by contrast, "*walks, labors and sleeps in the sunlight unharmed"*(430). The speech ignores Douglass's own history and identity: Forty years earlier he had fled north to freedom; he migrated further north to Rochester, where he spent the most productive years of life; and he enthusiastically endorsed the "exodus" of 3,000 poor, mostly urban blacks to the cold Adirondack mountains to become independent, landowning farmers on 120,000 acres that Gerrit Smith had given them.[41]

Douglass downplays his identity as a black man when he describes his second marriage in the 1892 edition of *Life and Times*. In 1884, after his first wife Anna Murray died, he married Helen Pitts— his secretary who was twenty years his junior. His marriage did not symbolize (at least in his mind) a radical interracial and egalitarian union. He describes it not as an interracial union; rather, he says that he married someone lighter than him, *"of the complexion of my father rather than[...]my mother"*(534).

Douglass's retreat from a position of racial equality after the war was not unique: in many respects it paralleled the retreat of many other abolitionists from their millennialist ideals and militant means before the war. After the war he continued to ascend socially— he got rich, became more famous, and was appointed to positions that had previously been reserved for whites. But his trajectory was not representative— he had been a "*representative man*" by speaking and fighting for black interests, and in representing what was possible, but not as a synecdoche of black conditions. His ascent after Reconstruction shrouded him (and whites) from the nation's abandonment of legal freedom and its retreat from egalitarian ideals. Douglass also relinquished the ideal of racial equality in *Life and Times*, even though he represented himself as a free man. His sublime black aesthetic was replaced by a desublimated, beautiful white one.[42]

Douglass's formal and political radicalism in *My Bondage and My Freedom*, and throughout his writings, speeches, and actions in the 1850s, stemmed from his struggle to collapse cultural dichotomies that had long served as a source of order and hierarchy and posed obstacles to the new age: black and white, heaven and earth; civilization and

---

[41] See Stauffer, *Black Hearts of Men*, pp. 134-181, 277-281.

[42] Hans Kellner notes that the shift from sublime to the beautiful in historical studies did not mean *"a flight from ugliness,"* for *"the last two centuries offer as much horror, atrocity, indecency, and strife as any other period."* Rather, "beautiful history" focused on the real experience, dispassionate discourse, and a moral high ground. See Kellner, "However Imperceptibly: From the Historical to the Sublime," p. 592.

savagery; and masculine and feminine. To these I would add the dichotomies of art and politics, subject and object. The concept of empathy, which was crucial to Douglass's reform vision, appropriately has aesthetic roots. Empathy stems from the German word, "Einfühlung," and was first used in 1872 to describe abstraction and subjectivity in theories of art, whereby the subject (or viewer) identifies so closely with the feelings evoked by the art object (or image) that subject and object get blurred— the viewer seeks to become one with the image.[43]

Douglass was not always successful in collapsing these dichotomies, particularly masculine and feminine. He was the foremost male feminist of his day, and Elizabeth Cady Stanton called him the only man who really understood what it felt like to be disenfranchised. Douglass spoke at the 1848 Seneca Falls Convention, and helped save from defeat the resolution on woman's suffrage, which many attenders viewed as too radical.[44] But he had difficulty representing women— especially black women— as performative or artistic selves. For him, as well as for Kant, sublime representations were typically masculine.[45] He kept his representations of women to his private rather than public imagination.

Douglass nevertheless went further than his peers in trying to blur and collapse these dichotomies in the 1850s. By attacking the Aristotelian belief that some men were born to rule, and others to serve and do the basic work of society, he and his comrades were led to question other dichotomies — as opposed to more conservative reformers and artists, who contained their assault and legitimated the status quo by separating slavery from other institutions. In striving to break down these

---

[43] Charles Edward Gauss,"Empathy," *Dictionary of the History of Ideas*, ed. Philip M. Wiener (New York: Charles Scribner's Sons, 1973), pp. 85-89; Stauffer, *Black Hearts of Men*, pp. 1-7, 14-20, 38-40.

[44] Philip S. Foner, ed., *Frederick Douglass on Women's Rights* (1976, reprint, New York: Da Capo Press, 1992), p. ix, 1-14; Stauffer, *Black Hearts of Men*, pp. 224-232.

[45] Kant associates masculine qualities with "*deep understanding*, an expression that signifies identity with the sublime." See Kant, *Observations on the Feeling of the Beautiful and Sublime*, pp. 77, 78.

dichotomies, Douglass continually refashioned himself at the same time he sought to reform the country. He moved beyond an understanding of "character" that was fixed, unchanging, and based primarily on heredity and social status, and embraced a highly subjective notion of the self that was in a state of continual flux. The idea of "whiteness" as a sign of superiority, a marker of social status, and a justification for racial oppression depended on an understanding of character that was fixed and unchanging.

After the war, he gradually retreated from his vision of social leveling and militancy, both aesthetically and ideologically. It was as though the apocalypse had come, but the new age was nowhere in sight. As a result, a heaven on earth increasingly seemed to him a sentimental illusion. He became more secular in his worldview, renounced his faith in the sublime as the appropriate mode for representing himself and freedom, and no longer believed that God could change the world or affect the laws of nature. In *Life and Times* he castigates blacks for believing that they could procure *"help from the Almighty"*(480). By remaining true to their faith, blacks were "false" to fact and thus to history, he argued (480). Material facts and the laws of nature now trumped *"all the prayers of Christendom"* (479). With his religious backsliding came a reversal of his aesthetic beliefs: he embraced progressive history over *kairos* (a sharp break from the past); rationality over emotion; and beauty and reason over the sublime power of the imagination.

WORKS CITED

Aristotle. *Poetics.* Trans. and Ed. Malcolm Heath. New York: Penguin Books, 1996.

Aristotle. *The Politics.* Trans. Sinclair, T.A. New York: Penguin Books, 1981.

Barton, Anne. "Not an Ideal Husband." *The New York Review of Books* November 18, 1999: 46.

Blight, David. Ed. *Narrative of the Life of Frederick Douglass, An American Slave.* Boston and New York: Bedford/St. Martins, 2nd ed., 2003.

Boyer, Peter J. "Ron Brown's Secrets." *The New Yorker*, June 9, 1997: 67.

Burke, Edmund. *A Philosophical Enquiry into the Origin of Our Ideas of the Sublime and Beautiful.* Ed. J.T. Boulton (1958; reprint). Notre Dame: University of Notre Dame Press, 1968.

Davis, David Brion. *The Problem of Slavery in Western Culture.* New York: Oxford University Press, 1966.

Davis, David Brion. *In the Image of God: Religion, Moral Values, and Our Heritage of Slavery.* New Haven: Yale University Press, 2001.

Douglass, F. "A Tribute for the Negro." Ed. Philip Foner. *The Life and Writings of Frederick Douglass, vol. 1.*

Douglass, F. "From the Editor." *The North Star.* November 23, 1849.

Douglass, F. *Life and Times of Frederick Douglass, Written by Himself.* New York: Collier Books, 1962.

Douglass, F. *My Bondage and My Freedom.* Ed. William L. Andrews (1855; reprint). Urbana: University of Illinois Press, 1987.

Douglass, F. "Persecution on Account of Faith, Persecution on Account of Color: An Address . . . on 26 January 1851." Ed. Blassingame. *Frederick Douglass Papers*, series 1, volume 2. New Haven: Yale University Press, 1982.

Douglass, F. "Pictures and Progress." Ed. John Blassingame. *The Frederick Douglass Papers, series 1, volume 3*. New Haven: Yale University Press, 1985.

Douglass, F. "Pictures." holograph, n.d. [late 1864]. *Frederick Douglass Papers.* Washington: Library of Congress.

Douglass, F. *The Heroic Slave.* Ed. Ronald T. Takaki. *Violence in the Black Imagination: Essays and Documents, Expanded Edition.* New York: Oxford University Press, 1993.

Douglass, F. "The Day of Jubilee Comes." Ed. Blassingame. *The Frederick Douglass Papers.* 1:3.

Du Bois, W. *The Souls of Black Folk.* New York: Penguin Books,1989.

Ed. Foner, Philip S. *Frederick Douglass on Women's Rights* (1976, reprint). New York: Da Capo Press, 1992.

Gates, Henry Louis Jr. "The Trope of a New Negro and the Reconstruction of the Image of the Black." Ed. Philip Fisher. *The New American Studies: Essays from Representations.* Berkeley: University of California Press, 1991.

Gauss, Charles Edward. "Empathy." Ed. Philip M. Wiener. *Dictionary of the History of Ideas.* New York: Charles Scribner's Sons, 1973.

Ed.Vicki Goldberg. *Photography in Print: Writings from 1816 to the Present.* Albuquerque: University of New Mexico Press, 1981.

Hawthorne, Nathaniel. *The House of Seven Gables.* New York: The New American Library, 1961.

Eds. H. J. Jackson and J.R.de J. Jackson. *The Collected Works of Samuel Taylor Coleridge, vol. 11: Shorter Works and Fragments, vol. 1.* Princeton: Princeton University Press, 1995.

Kant, Immanuel *Observations on the Feeling of the Beautiful and Sublime.* Tr. John T. Goldthwait. Berkeley: University of California Press, 1960.

Kellner, Hans. "However Imperceptibly: From the Historical to the Sublime." *PMLA* 118:3 (May 2003): 591-596.

Mitchell, W. J. T. *Iconology: Image, Text, Ideology.* Chicago: University of Chicago Press, 1986.

Nadar. "Balzac and the Daguerreotype." *Literature and Photography: Interactions, 1840-1990.* Ed. Jane M. Rabb. Albuquerque: University of New Mexico Press, 1995.

Proceedings of the Convention of Radical Political Abolitionists, Held at Syracuse, New York, June 26th, 27th, and 28th, 1855. New-York: Central Abolition Board, 1855.

Quarles, Benjamin. *Frederick Douglass* (1948; reprint). New York: Da Capo Press,1997.

Rogers, Nathaniel P. "Southern Slavery and Northern Religion." Feb. 1, 1844, reprinted in Ed.David Blight. *Narrative of the Life of Frederick Douglass, An American Slave.* Bedford/St. Martins, 2nd ed., 2003.

Scarry, E. *On Beauty and Being Just.* Princeton: Princeton University Press, 1999.

Stauffer, John. *The Black Hearts of Men: Radical Abolitionists and the Transformation of Race* Cambridge: Harvard University Press, 2002.

Stauffer, John and McCarthy, Timothy *Millennial Vistas: New Essays on Abolitionism.* New York: The Free Press, 2004.

Stepto, Robert. "Storytelling in Early Afro-American Fiction: Frederick Douglass's 'The Heroic Slave.'" *Georgia Review* 36 (1982): 355-368.

Stowe, Harriet Beecher. *Uncle Tom's Cabin; or, Life Among the Lowly.* New York: Penguin Books, 1981.

Voss, Frederick S. *Majestic in His Wrath: A Pictorial Life of Frederick Douglass.* Washington, D.C.: Smithsonian Institution Press, 1995.

Weiskel, Thomas *The Romantic Sublime: Studies in the Structure and Psychology of Transcendence.* Baltimore: Johns Hopkins University Press, 1976.

Wiedemann, Thomas. *Greek and Roman Slavery.* London: Routledge, 1994.

Wolf, Bryan J. *Romantic Re-Vision: Culture and Consciousness in Nineteenth-Century American Painting and Literature.* Chicago: University of Chicago Press, 1982.

I.2 Obododimma Oha: In Lucifer We Trust: Reading William Blake's Reading of America's Mythical History

"Empire is no more! and now the lion & wolf shall cease"
-- William Blake, *Song of Liberty*

***

Washington Irving, who is believed to be the father of American literature, in his *Rip Van Winkle, a Posthumous Writing of Diedrich Knickerbocker* (1819), (re)tells the story of the Dutch American, Rip Van Winkle, who drank some flagon liquor and fell asleep at the supposedly enchanted Kaastkill Mountains in Hudson in America when the country was still a colony of the British Empire. The man woke up from his sleep twenty years later (which was to him just a night gone) to discover that he had become an unrecognisable stranger in his own community, a strangeness that made him suspect in the eyes of the tavern politicians who immediately required him to declare his political affiliation. Gripped by fear, Rip Van Winkle in his innocence cried:

"Alas! Gentlemen[...]I am a poor, quiet man, a native of the place, and a loyal subject of the king, God bless him!" (Irving 1980: 74).

The instant angry response from the bystanders to this verbalization of loyalty to a past that belonged to the Empire was: *"A tory! A tory! A spy! A refugee! Hustle him! Away with him!"* (74). Rip Van Winkle had fallen asleep in the Time of the Empire and had woken up in the Time of the Republic, and so still had the memory and the fear of the Empire.

Between my reading of the story and William Blake's reading of America's mythical history lies an encounter with a changing American image. William Blake's long epic poem, *America: A Prophecy* (written 1793), provides a powerful evidence of the visualization and verbalization of America in ways that involve a spiritualization and re/mythologizing of history. The concern of this chapter is to explore this spiritualization and re/mythologizing of American history, especially in relation to the American confrontation with British imperialism. The chapter will try to show that Blake reconstructs the history of America, turning American leaders and revolutionaries into mythical protagonists, and indeed re-imagining the American context in ways that insert the exotic and the gothic within a visualized empire of grandeur.[1] The chapter reads Blake as poetically producing a grand narrative in which America is figured as a continuation and complementation of Europe and it also discusses this myth of historical and cultural continuation, relating it to the imagination of America not as being just the "New World" but as the "New Europe". Then it asks a question: Is America anything more than a poem written to be read as the already-written in the European past?

The discovery, the founding, and the defence of America, and even the creation of an *American* future, have been interesting sources of grand narratives, as witnessed in accounts by (Christian) explorers like Christopher Columbus, the early Puritan immigrants, the Mormons, and more recently in video documentaries and films by Christian revivalists of American innocence.[2] America emerges in these grand narratives as the "Earthly Paradise" (Columbus), or the "Promised Land" (Columbus, Mormon), the "New Jerusalem" or the "City upon a Hill" (as in the case of

---

[1] William Blake's visual illustrations in the poem reinforce the act of myth-making, especially in terms of the enlistment of the powers of vision and imagination to narrate the entity. Blake was a great painter who, as Morris Eaves (1993:237) notes, epitomizes the Romantic multi-talentedness, and most of his poems could be seen as a "painting" of profound experience. Indeed, Blake appeared to be demythologising the relationship between the Word and the pictorial image; he dismantles the modal difference and reconstructs a new myth of interarts communication. Perhaps the fact that right from childhood he started seeing visions (Claire 1992:255) was an influence on this inclination towards exploring modes of "painting" the profound experience.

[2] Columbus, in the narrative of his third voyage, says of the New World: *"For I believe that the earthly paradise lies here, which no one can enter except by God's leave"* (220-221). Interestingly, he is referred to in *The First Book of Nephi* 13:12, in *The Book of Mormon* as a man elected by God from among the Gentiles to get in touch with the elect "who were in the promised land". Christian documentaries, for instance Richard Blair's *In God We Trust* and *The Incredible Power of Prayer*, reinforce the myths of America as a divinely created idea.

the Puritans), each of these identifications suggesting a myth and an utopia of some divine plan, and intertextually deriving from Biblical grand narratives . Each of the (foundational) narratives constructs America as a land of liberty (or freedom), where this liberty is again understood as being divinely created and maintained. Interestingly too, even the British Imperial power that colonized and ruled America invoked some divine legitimation, as for instance in the divine right of His/Her Majesty, which must be respected by even by a (colonized) subject just waking up from a twenty-year slumber.

Given the power and dominance of grand narratives that spiritualize America, there appears to be a sufficient basis for William Blake's attempt at creating what Friedrich Schlegel (cited in M.H. Abrams' *Natural Supernaturalism* 67) refers to as a "new mythology" on the history of American liberation in his epic poem, *America: A Prophecy*, which he published in 1793. Of course, Blake himself had, early in his career as a poet and an artist, had a significant rendezvous with radical European theologians and millenarian groups, including the Swedenborgians, which must have sufficiently fired his radical apocalyptic posture. Also, the Romantic Movement in Europe generally appropriated religious ideals and postures in its quest for a better society. As Abrams informs us in *Natural Supernaturalism*, philosophers and creative thinkers who wrote in the era of the French Revolution were much inclined to metaphysics, *and "considered themselves as elected spokesmen for the Western tradition at a time of profound cultural crisis,"* and thus

They represented themselves in the traditional persona of the philosopher-seer or the poet-prophet[...] and they set out, in various yet recognizably parallel ways, to reconstitute the grounds of hope and to announce the certainty, or at least the possibility, of a rebirth in which a renewed mankind will inhabit a renovated earth where he will find himself thoroughly at home"(Abrams 1973: 12).

Abrams writes that the orientation of secular thinkers during the Romantic period in Europe was not that of *"the deletion and replacement of religious ideas but rather the assimilation and reinterpretation of religious ideas, as constitutive elements in a world view founded on secular premises"* (13).

Thus we find that some of the writings of the Romantics like Blake create intersections between history, religion, and politics, often interrogating their discourses on truth, in line with what Michel Foucault was to do later in his deconstructive project on historical truth in *Nietzsche, Genealogy, History.* Abrams again explains that works like William Blake's *America: A Prophecy*, *Europe: A Prophecy*, *Song of Liberty*, and Samuel Taylor Coleridge's *Religious Musings* and *Destiny of Nations*, which appropriate the ancient persona of the poet-prophet " *'the Bard', who present, past, and future sees*", do

"incorporate the great political events of their age in suitably grandiose literary forms, especially the epic and 'the greater Ode'; they present a panoramic view of history in a cosmic setting, in which the agents are in part historical and in part allegorical or mythological and the overall design is apocalyptic; they envision a dark past, a violent present, and an immediately impending future which will justify the history of suffering man by its culmination in an absolute good" (332).

Very clearly, Blake's preoccupation in *America: A Prophecy* is to reinvent the liberation myth, blasphemously recreating Lucifer or Satan as the author and patron of American freedom.

In *America: A Prophecy*, Blake is celebrating this freedom, this new mythology, beginning his own grand narrative in the *Preludium* to the poem with a telling sexual encounter between Orc (Satan) and the "dark virgin" (symbolizing America), the sexual ravishing of the virgin reminding us again about Amerigo Vespucci's mythical configuration of the New World as a virgin waiting to be ravished, or as a lady who, even after several childbirths, remains highly desirable and sensuous. Orc initiates his project through this symbolic coitus, giving the virgin life, freedom, and happiness, as she later announces. This freedom, as revealed later in the main poem by George Washington, is threatened by the oppressive (spiritual) forces operating from Albion's shore:

> *"Washington spoke: "Friends of America, look over the Atlantic sea;*
> *A bended bow is lifted in heaven, & a heavy iron chain*
> *Descends link by link from Albion's cliffs across the sea to bind*
> *Brothers & sons of America, till our faces pale and yellow,*
> *Heads deprest, voices weak, eyes downcast, hands work-bruis'd,*
> *Feet bleeding on the sultry sands, and the furrows of the whip*
> *Descend to generations that in future times forget"*
> (Blake 1970).

Among the voices and mythologized protagonists used in the poem, Washington speaks to rouse Americans and the "friends of America" against the threat on the nation.The warning against the descent of the "heavy iron chain" which is meant "to bind / Brothers & sons of America" applies not only to the reality of British colonization, but also to the future (threat to America); in other words, the future of the nation hinges on the vision (of freedom) at its foundation. Blake (in Washington's voice) already invokes the significance of memory in the making of the nation: *"[...] and the furrows of the whip/ Descend to generations that in future times forget".*

Perhaps we should bring Homi Bhabha into this: In his famous essay, *DissemiNation: Time, narrative and the margins of the modern nation* (Bhabha 139-170), Bhabha writes about the importance of the "*syntax of forgetting— or being obliged to forget*" in "*the construction of the national present*" (160). But this is paradoxical in the American case. While being "*obliged to forget*" might well work out in the integration of the African-Americans and the Native Americans into the "*nation of nations*"— so that this nation of nations remains dominant— it is difficult for the nation to pursue or remain within the ambience of its ideology (of creating freedom) if its members suffer from amnesia in respect of *using* the nation's foundational history. So, the nation is located between forgetting and remembering, always.

In the poem, the Sceptre (Orc) that arises to announce freedom to America seems to reinforce the spiritualization of America's foundation and existence. In his Christian documentaries on the history of America called *The Power of Prayer* and *In God We Trust*, Richard Blair has clearly identified the defeat of the British forces and the victory of America in all its other wars and conflicts (right from the foundation of the nation) as acts of God, reinforcing the idea of the founding and the continuity of America as the fulfilment of God's divine will (Oha). In the documentaries too, Washington is mythologized as the invincible and invulnerable spirit that guards the American nation. In *America: A Prophecy*, the Spectre in "*beams of blood*" and frightening even Albion's "*wrathful Prince*", brings the message of freedom, after Washington has spoken, much as the announcement of the Resurrection:

> *"The morning comes, the night decays, the watchmen leave their stations,*
> *The grave is burst, the spices shed, the linen wrapped up;*
> *The bones of death, the covering clay, the sinews shrunk & dry'd*
> *Reviving shake, inspiring move, breathing! awakening!*
> *Spring like redeemed captives when their bones & bars are burst.*
> *Let the slave grinding at the mill run out into the field,*
> *Let him look up into the heavens & laugh in the bright air:*
> *Let the inchained soul, shut up in darkness and in sighing,*

Whose face has never seen a smile in thirty weary years,
Rise and look out; his chains are loose, his dungeon doors are open,
And let his wife and children return from the oppressor's scourge.
They look behind at every step & believe it is a dream,
Singing: 'The sun has left his blackness, & has found a fresher morning,
And the fair Moon rejoices in the clear and cloudless night;
For Empire is no more, and now the Lion & Wolf shall cease'" (lines 37-51).

The murky and cloudy "night" of the Empire and the "morning" of the free America (both archetypal metaphors of fear and hope respectively) constitute the very important issues. The night of the Empire is the captivity of the grave, the morning of America analogous to the Resurrection of Jesus Christ. In thinking of the liberation of America in Biblical/Christian images, Blake locates the being of the nation in the spiritual sphere.[3] Indeed, as Max Plowman has intimated us in his introduction to a collection of Blake's works, locating the political in the domain of the spiritual was in the character of Blake's commitment as an artist, Plowman states that *"The discovery of spiritual identities was Blake's idea of the poet's work"* (xvi), and also that

"The animating of all sensible objects with God or Geniuses is a very exact description of what Blake

[3] This spiritualization of the being of the nation appears to have parallels in some recent narratives about invasions of America by extra-terrestrial forces, the production of Nuclear missiles and attack on America by an Anti-Christ (from the Arab world), and the appropriations of the prophecies of Michel Nostradamus, which we find in some Hollywood American films. These appear to be insignificant, but they

> *attempted to do in all his longer work, and beginning with the human soul he discovered a variety of "Gods or Geniuses" (or what we should commonly call principles) active there. These gods, in their struggles for supremacy, carried on the wars of the spiritual world"*(Plowman xvi).

In William Blake's *America: A Prophecy*, agents like Orc, Urizen, and the "nameless" "shadowy daughter of Urthona" are allegorical and mythical figures, while Washington, Paine, Franklin, Warren, Gates, Hancock and Green are first of all known historical figures. However, located in the mythological context, these historical figures become part of the imagined spiritual and mythical experience. Blake seems to perceive allegorical figures like Orc as changing forces. In his editorial commentary in *The Norton Anthology of English Poetry*, Abrams explains that

"In Blake's later poems, Orc, the fiery spirit of revolution, gives way as a central personage to Los, the type of the visionary imagination in the fallen world",

and insists that

"Even in his early writings[...] Blake had represented historical revolution as a correlative with a radical change effected within the mind and imagination of man, so that replacement of Orc by Los does not indicate Blake's recantation of former beliefs, but a shift of emphasis from an apocalypse by revolution to an apocalypse by imagination" (Abrams 1973: 22).

In *America: A Prophecy*, what is enacted clearly is "*an apocalypse by revolution*", even though this revolution is mythical. Interestingly, the agent of this revolution is Orc, who, ironically, is identified as Lucifer and the Anti-Christ:

> *"Art thou not Orc, who serpent-formed*

---

may stimulate some primordial fears about the being and future of America as a "free" nation.

Stands at the gate of Enitharmon to devour her children,
Blasphemous Demon, Antichrist, hater of Dignities,
Lover of wild rebellion, and transgressor of God's Law"(line 54 - 57)

Or, as he identifies himself in response:

"I am Orc, wreath'd round the accursed tree.
The times are ended: shadows pass, the morning 'gins to break:
The fiery joy that Urizen perverted to ten commands
What night he led the starry hosts thro' the wild wilderness,
That stony law I stamp to dust, and scatter religion abroad
...
That pale religious lechery, seeking Virginity,
May find it in a harlot, and in coarse-clad honesty
The undefiled tho' ravish'd in her cradle night and morn;"(line 59 - 70)

Blake invents a "new mythology" which, though it derives from Biblical apocalypse and the *Genesis* myth of the Fall, is given a revolutionary direction. Lucifer, in the Biblical context, may well have claimed to be pursuing a revolutionary goal, undermining the authority of God and giving some freedom of choice to Adam and Eve, although the Christian view suggests this liberation as an attempt to mislead, to create their Death or Fall. Indeed, Satan's argument suggest this construction of the image of self as liberator:

"And the Serpent said to the woman, You shall not surely die: For God does know that in the day you eat thereof, then your eyes shall be

opened, and you shall be as god, knowing good and evil" (*Genesis* 3: 4-5).

The liberation is, interestingly, a project on knowledge creation, an issue that had led some ancient theologians to think that the pursuit of knowledge is inimical to healthy religious life, or that it is Satanic. Even *The Book of Proverbs* asserts that one cannot find God with the intellect.

Unlike the Puritans in early America who saw the founding of the nation as the establishment of a New Jerusalem, and perceived, in literal Biblical sense, the war that Satan wages against the foundation and existence of the nation, Blake makes Satan the one who frees the nation from domination and oppression. Assigning Satan this positive role is a paradox indeed: Orc or Satan now gives joy and life America the "Dark Virgin", having ravished her sexually, whereas in the Biblical context he tries to destroy the Virgin and her children:

> *"And there appeared a great wonder in heaven; a woman clothed with the sun, and the moon under her feet, and upon her head a crown of twelve stars: And she being with child cried, travailing in birth, and pained to be delivered. And there appeared another wonder in heaven; and behold a great red dragon having seven heads and ten horns, and seven crowns upon his heads. And his tail drew the third part of the stars of heaven, and did cast them to the earth; and the dragon stood before the woman which was ready to be delivered, for to devour her child as soon as it was born*"(Revelation 12:1- 4).

The Marian cult in the Catholic Church interprets this woman to be the Virgin Mary, and visually represents her celestial royalty referred to above (the crown of the twelve stars and the moon under her feet), even though this archetypal image has antecedents in pagan traditions. William

Blake rewrites the Biblical myths, so that the new (grand) narrative glorifies Satan. Just as in the case of Milton— whom Blake says

"wrote in fetters when he wrote of Angels & God, and at liberty when of Devils & Hell[...] because he was a true Poet and of the Devil's party without knowing it" (" The Voice of the Devil", *The Marriage of Heaven and Hell*) — Blake's Messiah is also "*called Satan*". Like other Romantics who subscribed to the (textual) strategy of contradiction, Blake believes that

"Without Contraries is no progression. Attraction and Repulsion, Reason and Energy, Love and Hate, are necessary to Human existence"("The Argument", in *The Marriage of Heaven and Hell*).

Indeed, the investment of Satan with messianic and revolutionary attributes, especially in the context of liberating America, is an exemplification of the marriage of "Heaven" and "Hell". Blake's revolutionary Satan indeed claims that "*The times are ended*", the old myth has been replaced with a new one— the new myth of himself is now the positive, not the negative one in the Christian master narrative.

Already always a rebel, Orc the terror, the Serpent, is reborn:

> *"... Ah rebel form that rent the ancient*
> *Heavens! Eternal Viper self-renew'd, rolling in clouds,*
> *I see thee in thick clouds and darkness on America's*
> *shore*
> *Writhing in pangs of abhorred birth[...]"*(line 90 - 93).

And so Albion's Angel raises an alarm, calling his "Thirteen Angels" to rise to battle against this threat. The "Thirteen Angels" rule the thirteen states/provinces of British America at the spiritual realm. They are alternatively referred to " guardians" of these colonies. From Blake's mythical geography, these guardian Angels of the colonies (that spiritually enforce colonial domination) operate from a liminal space, from a space in-between a lost portion of the earth and America the New World; in-between a kingdom-gone and a kingdom-come:

> *"On those vast shady hills between America & Albion's shore*
> *Now barr'd out by the Atlantic sea, call'd Atlantean hills*
> *Because from their bright summits you may pass to the Golden world,*
> *An ancient palace, archetype of mighty Emperies,*
> *Rears its immortal pinnacles, built in the forest of God*
> *By Ariston the king of beauty for his stolen bride.*
> *Here on their magic seats the thirteen Angels sat perturbe'd,*
> *For clouds from the Atlantic hover o'er the solemn roof*"(line 107 - 114).

To be located in between the Then and the Now is already suggestive of a dislocation. The dislocation, the displacement and replacement of the colonizer, is even made irrevocable by the violence the colonizer enacts—a violence against the Other that consumes the Self. So, as in the case of the British who tried to crush the idea of self-determination in America (the idea couched in the American *Declaration of Independence*), when Albion's Angel cries repeatedly: *" Sound! Sound! My loud war-trumpets & alarm my Thirteen Angels!"* he signals the ominous, ironically. Interestingly, "Thirteen" is perceived in Western superstition (?) as a bad number, as a numeral signifier of ill luck or tragedy. From the "Ideas of March" (13 March) to the (skipped) 13th floor of high-rise buildings, we find this narrative of tragedy and fear written on the Western mind, which is possibly a semiotic invoked by Blake in the reiteration of "thirteen". Of course, there is something seemingly occult about Blake's archetypal representations generally.

The rebellion of the thirteen Angels, led by Boston's Angel, generally precipitates fear and disorder among the thirteen colonial governors and the British soldiers in the thirteen states (the earthly agents of the spiritual oppression). The soldiers, confronted by the *"visions of Orc"* and the flames, *"threw their swords and muskets to the earth & ran / From their encampments and dark castles, seeking where to hide ..."* (line 147-150). The plagues released on America by Albion's Angel and his numerous hosts almost destroy the country, forcing

"The citizens of New-York (to) close their books & lock their chests", " *The mariners of Boston (to) drop their anchors and unlade"*, *"The scribe of Pennsylvania"* to cast " *his pen upon the earth"*, and *"The builder of Virginia"* to throw *"his hammer down in fear"* (line 170 -173). This would have meant the loss of America (just like Atlantis), which, according to Blake, would have been a great tragedy to the world. But, as a kind of retributive justice, the plagues turn to attack their senders, reinforced by the "*burning winds driven by the flames of Orc"*. The Sprit of London is struck by Leprosy, while Bristol's is struck by the spotted plague. Even Urizen, "*who sat / Above all heavens in thunders wrapp'd*", is attacked by Leprosy, and

> *"... his tears in deluge piteous*
> *Falling into the deep sublime; flag'd with grey-brow'd snows*
> *And thunderous visages, his jealous wings wav'd over the deep;*
> *Weeping in dismal howling woe, he dark descended, howling*
> *Around the smitten bands, clothed in tears & trembling shud'ring cold.*
> *His stored snows he poured forth, and his icy magazines*
> *He open'd on the deep and on the Atlantic sea white shiv'ring.*
> *Leprous his limbs, all over white, and hoary was his visage,*

Weeping in dismal howlings before the stern Americans... "(line 207- 215).

The "*bands of Albion*" and *"the ancient Guardians"* are forced to seek refuge in *"their law-built heaven"*, but as they try to shut the five gates for security, these gates are also *"consumed & their bolts and hinges melted"*.

Urizen, in this epic, is made a collaborator in oppression and colonization, and is also a victim. The Imperial Heaven is thus prophesied as something that would be destroyed by its own instruments. Obviously, Blake is referring to the circumstances that led to the collapse of the British rule in America, and to the defeat of Britain by America in the American War of Independence. The Empire, in the memory of the American nation, is understandably a horror; to forget its meaning, as Washington states in the poem, is to return to oppression. In this case, if Empire and the colonies are *absences*, they are also forces that engage in the production of the meaning of America as the land of liberty (which is also an alternative myth competing with other myths).

A "world-builder", as he is referred to by Marilyn Butler, William Blake's visualization and verbalization of America through the epic tries to imagine a new future for Europe. In this case, America would be a continuation of Europe, not through colonization (which has now failed), not as EU/ropean satellite, but through the meaning and direction it gives to Europe. The American Revolution, as Butler states, *"was a great issue and source of radical stimulus in Continental Europe"* (15). At the intellectual level, many European thinkers, back in time, had recognized the significance of America as a "new" Europe. Humboldt, for *instance,*

"Unlike Erasmus or Cardano, unlike even Condercet[...] was convinced that the discovery of America had 'multiplied the objects of knowledge and man's contemplation' to the point where he had been driven to adopt a new mental stance to cope with information now available to him" (Pagden 1993: 113).

Explaining further, Pagden cites Humboldt as arguing that before the discovery of America,

"the intellectual progress of (European) man had been determined by his capacity to respond to 'external occurrences'", and so his intellect was *"constrained precisely by what he knew about his natural environment"*. However,

"once America had been added to the 'objects of contemplation' now available to the European scientific gaze, the intellect 'henceforth produces[...]grand results by its own peculiar and internal power in every direction at the same time'. Once, that is, it had grasped the significance of its collective encounter with the New World, the human intellect had begun to operate in new and distinctly modern ways"(Pagden 1993:114).

America: A Prophecy was published a year before *Europe: A Prophecy* (1794), but both poems exist in complementary relationship, just as Europe and America might be thought to complement each other. Indeed, the two may be said to constitute the same narrative on the *"struggle between liberty and despotism"* (Dawson 1996:51). Enitharmon's children — Orc, Los, Rintrah, Palamabron, Elynittria, and Ocalythron — summoned by her, still confront Albion's Angel's who are struck by their own plagues, in *Europe: A Prophecy*. But this time, Europe is the site of the battle. At the end of the poem, it is Los that now takes over as the revolutionary figure, calling out *"all his sons to the strife of blood"* in the "*vineyards of France"* (line 200- 208). The American Revolution and the French Revolution are therefore connected by the poet. Abrams notes that, as *"an ardent supporter of the French Revolution"*, Blake,

"like Wordsworth, Coleridge, Southey, and a number of radical English theologians, represented the contemporary the contemporary Revolution as the purifying violence that, according to Biblical prophecy, was the portent of the imminent redemption of humanity and the world"

(Editorial commentary in *The Norton Anthology of English Poetry* 1986: 22).

America, to the Romantics like Blake, is no longer to be understood as the "New World" waiting to be dominated, but a "new" world because it brings the necessity for liberty to the world. It is for them a "New Europe", not because it is a new space for European domination and exploitation, but a space that enables Europe to articulate its progressive Self. Very recently there was a heated debate in the European American Studies Association as to whether going to Graz, Austria, to hold the Association's meeting was morally, politically, and intellectually appropriate, given the new role that Mr Haider has been allowed to play in Austrian politics and government. It would appear that the Association was hiding behind the symbolism of Haider to enact the value of America as an object of study. America appears to mean the "New Europe" that has memory and vision for liberty, and so America is already written, is already a given, to European intellectual reflection. This given-ness of America is the problem: What are the possibilities, and indeed the implications, of making America, as a poem already-written in the European past, begin to yield multiple meanings, even contrary meanings, as in Blake's idea that *"Without Contraries is not progression"*?

WORKS CITED

Abrams, M. H. *Natural Supernaturalism: Tradition and Revolution in Romantic Literature*. New York: W. W. Norton & Co., 1973.

Abrams, M. H. Editorial commentary in *The Norton Anthology of English Poetry*. Ed. M. H. Abrams. New York/ W. W. Norton & Co., 1986. 20-88.

Bhabha, Homi K. *The Location of Culture* (rpt). London & New York: Routledge, 1995.

Blair, Richard. *In God We Trust* & *The Power of Prayer. The Incredible Power of Prayer* Vols. 1 & 2. Loveland: Group Productions, n.d.

Blake, William. *America: A Prophecy. Poems and Prophecies*. New York: Dent, 1793/1970. 63-69.

Blake, William. *The Marriage of Heaven and Hell. Poems and Prophecies*, rpt 1793/1970. 42-55.

Blake, William. *Europe: A Prophecy. Poems and Prophecies*, 1794/1970. 70-77.

Book of Mormon, The. Trans. Joseph Smith Jnr. Salt Lake City: The Church of Jesus Christ of Latter-Day Saints, 1973.

Butler, Marilyn. *Romantics, Rebels and Reactionaries: English Literature and its Background, 1760 - 1830*. Oxford: Oxford UP, 1981.

Claire, Lamont. "The Romantic Period". *An Outline of English Literature*. Ed. Pat Rogers .Oxford: Oxford UP, 1992. 250-298.

Columbus, Christopher. *The Four Voyages of Christopher Columbus*. Ed. & Trans. J. M. Cohen. London: Penguin, 1969.

Dawson, P. M. S. "Poetry in an Age of Revolution". *The Cambridge Companion to British Romanticism*. Ed. Stuart Curran. Cambridge: Cambridge UP, 1996. 48-73.

Eaves, Morris. "The Sister Arts in British Romanticism". *The Cambridge Companion to British Romanticism*. Ed. Stuart Curran. New York: Cambridge University Press. 230-269.

Foucault, Michel. "Nietzsche, Genealogy, History". *Language, Counter-Memory, Practice: Selected Essays and Interviews*. Ed. Donald F. Bouchard. Ithaca, NY: Cornel UP, 1977.204-217.

Genesis. (n.d.) *Holy Bible* (King James Version). Florida: The Publisher.

Irving, Washington. "Rip Van Winkle, A Posthumous Writing of Diedrich Knickerbocker". *The Legend of Sleepy Hollow and Rip Van Winkle.* USA: Watermill Press, 1819/1980.

Oha, Obododimma. "Documenting the Future of the American Past: Christian Visualization of the American Success". Paper presented at the International Conference of the French Association of American Studies, on "America as Image", Aix-en-Provence, France, 26-28 May, 2000.

Pagden, Anthony. *European Encounters with the New World: From Renaissance to Romanticism.* New Haven & London: Yale UP, 1993.

Revelation. (n.d.) Holy Bible (King James Version). Florida: The Publisher.

I.3 Anton Pokrivčák: Ontological as Aesthetic in Emily Dickinson's Poetry

In their well-known book *The Meaning of Meaning,* C. K. Ogden and I. A. Richards began their discussion of the phenomenon of meaning by quoting, among others, the late Dr. Postgate as saying that

"Throughout the whole history of the human race, there have been no questions that have caused more heart-searchings, tumults and devastation than questions of the correspondence of words to facts" (Ogden, Richards 1946: 2).

In literary studies, the questions of meaning have indeed been with us since the times of Aristotle and, in spite of that, have not stopped eclipsing the nature of literary art even in the third millennium. Their latest significant re-evaluation occurred in the late twentieth century, during a period that has loosely been called postmodernism. I will try to show that the postmodern contribution to this debate showed limits of one way of thinking and, as a consequence of this, initiated a new re-evaluation of older ones.

What seems to face its limits in the late stage of postmodernism is the seeing of reality through relativistic eyes. It is gradually becoming clear that the absolute citationality of the linguistic sign, as emphasised by Jacques Derrida and his followers, cannot be further developed, only degenerated. That it is so became evident when, out of necessity, a majority of the so-called postmodernists or poststructuralists took opportunity to use, or rather abuse, the semiotic nature of the linguistic sign for the enforcement of ideological claims. There is no doubt that, alongside their ideologising, they also managed to overthrow not a few dogmas. However, what has been once considered a strong point— the assumed absolute relativity that was to serve as an instrument to destroy traditional orthodox philosophical and literary principles, has become a drawback. A dramatic example of the degeneration was the so-called "Sokal Affair" which exposed this language as being rather a pure rhetoric in its classic, sophistic manifestation (*doxa*) than a knowledge based on the supporting evidence of facts derived from a serious study of reality, be it even a literary reality. It was brought to the public by the physicist Alan Sokal who sent to a leading journal of cultural studies, *Social Text*, an article entitled *Transgressing the Boundaries: Toward a Transformative Hermeneutics of Quantum Gravity* in which he claimed the following:

"*It has thus become increasingly apparent that physical 'reality', no less than social 'reality', is at bottom a social and linguistic construct; that scientific 'knowledge', far from being objective, reflects and encodes the dominant ideologies and power relations of the culture that produced it; that the truth claims of science are inherently theory-laden and self-referential; and consequently, that the discourse of the scientific community, for all its undeniable value, cannot assert a privileged epistemological status with respect to counter-hegemonic narratives emanating from dissident or marginalised communities*"(Sokal, 1996).

At first glance, there is nothing unusual about Sokal's language. It seems to be in line with the diction of most other articles in the (ideological) field, since the phrases like "*linguistic construct*", "*dominant ideology*", "*power structures*", "*hegemonic narratives*", "*marginalised communities*", have become the body of almost every article exploring, or drawing on, the postmodern condition of knowledge. What is uncommon about it, though, is the fact that it is, as Donald Freeman described it (1998:74), "*a complete hoax*", an article with, to use the postmodern terminology, no referential value. After its publication, the author in another journal openly declared that he mechanically put together various statements, without any supporting evidence, with the aim to find out whether

"*a leading North American journal of cultural studies[...][would] publish an article liberally salted with nonsense if (a) it sounded good and (b) it flattered the editors' ideological preconceptions*" (Freeman 1998: 74).

Despite an outbreak of understandable anger and, perhaps, rightful discussion of ethical dimension of Sokal's acting, the whole matter can be taken as a proof of, more than anything else so far, the superficiality of the relativistic-ideological approach to literature, since it has turned critical thinking into a play of childish, arbitrary statements. One of the consequences of "Sokal's affair" was a gradual strengthening of the voices calling for a theory which would take literature as an act of communication that may indeed refer "*to a phenomenal world*" as well as

"*aim at what may lie behind the wall of phenomena— as Moby Dick seeks to tell us something about a real whaling industry and the behavior of real whales and whalers, while also probing deeper into the mysteries of the universe*"(Scholes 1982: 24).

The new voices argue that without such theory literature would loose its most essential dimension, the ability to comment significantly on human life and to express fundamental human ethical values, for the "postmodern" academy

"*makes the language of power, colonization or marginalization replace the language of good, ought, and bad*" (Gregory, 1998).

In the next part of this chapter I would like to demonstrate, above all, the universality of such "*deep probing into the mysteries of the universe*" on some poems by Emily Dickinson and Wallace Stevens.

Emily Dickinson was a poet who drew on a relatively easily identifiable source of inspiration— a deep anxiety experienced during her life spent mostly in her parents' large country house. Although in its outward appearance that life must have been rather simple— based on what others would call "*a numbing routine*", in its inward quality it was a powerful volcano. In one of her poems she says it explicitly:

"*On my volcano grows the Grass / A meditative spot—* "(Dickinson 1989: 1677).

This image is perhaps the most exact figure characterizing her position in life, the position of someone tempting an abysmal and powerful depth. The perplexity and strangeness of her imagination may have been one of the reasons why she came to fame (or rather why fame came to her) only after her death and why her work has resisted all kinds of ideological appropriations so frequent in contemporary literary theory in general, and the American one in particular. To point to her "*exclusiveness*" and "*resistance to theory*" and ideology, I will make use of a rather longer quotation:

"[...]however celebrated her work on the part of poetry scholars, feminist critics, Americanists, and by contemporary women poets from Adrienne Rich to Susan Howe and Alice Fulton, Dickinson has never been what one might call the theorist's exemplary poet. Paradoxically, although there are now,[...] plenty of Lacanian, Foulcaultian, and Bakhtinian readings of Dickinson, her name nowhere appears in the indices of Lacan or Foucault or Bakhtin themselves. Indeed, you will not find Dickinson's name anywhere in the studies of Paul de Man or Jacques Derrida, in Julia Kristeva or Luce Irigaray, in Roland Barthes or Gilles Deleuze, in Michel Serres or Slavoj Žižek. Hélène Cixous, whose strong feminist/deconstructionist writings have addressed highly diverse writers—[...]— has had nothing whatever to say about Dickinson. Again, I have found no references to Dickinson in the writings of the Frankfurt School, or, more surprisingly, since these are Anglophone theorists, in the work of Raymond Williams or Terry Eagleton, Frank Kermode or Fredric Jameson" (Perloff 2000: 31-32).

Why is this so? Why can her poetry be celebrated and, at the same time, avoided, feared, ignored, resisted? One of the possible reasons has already been mentioned above— the perplexity of her imagination. As a person who was extremely separated from the rest of the world, both physically (living in a large country house only with her close relatives) and spiritually (communicating mostly with her consciousness and the things around her), she did not follow the usual road of versification, either in her themes or forms. As for the themes, the basic conflict of her poetry is between the experience and expression, between an implicit sense and an explicit form, between a sensed transcendental world and its closeness to a perceiving human mind, between life and death. Naturally, such thematic intensity (extreme introspection and variations on death occasionally giving way to warm and kind view) had to affect her composition as well (the desire to achieve gnomic compactness of expression frequently results in the disintegrated, fragmentary form). This, along with the potential danger, destruction, catastrophe, of the absolute knowledge, can be found in the following poem:

Tell all the Truth, but tell it slant—-
Success in Circuit lies
Too bright for our infirm Delight
The Truth's superb surprise

As Lightning to the Children eased
With explanation kind
The Truth must dazzle gradually
Or every man be blind
(Dickinson 1989:1116).

The poem says that truth has to be eased, it has to be accessed through mediating devices, signs. If this is not the case, we are blinded, dead, since no human withstands the authoritative essentiality of non-representational being. Such being is inaccessible, in its totality, to us since we are temporary beings, locked in time and space with only one possibility of escape— through the realm of non-being. The intimation of this (im)possibility allowed Dickinson to write poetry which is extraordinarily true, thematising essential facts of life in a human, non-essential way. Her poems are free of any dogmatic ideological or aesthetic totallsing conceptions. Instead, their essence lies in the interpretation of life both in its realistic simplicity as well as intellectual contradictoriness and sophistication. To follow the poet's sensation of being slowly forming itself through her poems requires from the reader to employ not only a significant amount of imaginative capacity, but considerable intellectual skills as well, forcing him/her to move on various levels of abstraction:

To be alive— is Power—
Existence— in itself—

Without a further function—
Omnipotence— Enough—

To be alive—and Will!
'Tis able as a God—
The Maker—of Ourselves— be what—
Such being Finitude! (Dickinson 1989: 1116).

The topic of this poem is obvious: the speaker is concerned with what is most fundamental about life: "to be alive", "power", "existence", "God", "will", "finitude". The poem begins by a relatively easy to understand identification of life with power— to be alive means to be powerful. However, in the next line we find that it is not a regular existence, but a phenomenological, transcendental stance. Such move, or rather "*a mode of being present* that at *once values and cancels the self*"(Hartman 1980:124) is typical of most of her poems. Because of this, she can be best described as a metaphysical poet who displays a great intensity of feeling for this world, trying to penetrate to its essential, constitutive parts. In her attempts, the consciousness is at the same time a light, focusing one's attention on the materiality of the things, on their being around us, as well as an eclipse hiding for ever their true nature.

This consciousness that is aware
Of neighbours and the Sun
Will be the one aware of Death
And that itself alone

Is traversing the interval
Experience between
And most profound experiment
Appointed unto Men-

How adequate unto itself

its properties shall be
Itself unto itself and none
Shall make discovery.

Adventure most unto itself
The Soul condemned to be—
Attended by a single Hound
Its own identity"
(Dickinson 1989: 1113 – 1114).

"*Traversing the interval*", moving "*in*" and "*out*" makes consciousness become her most intimate friend. It allows her wonder, meditate, analyse, and write— mostly in a non-separated manner. The relation of consciousness, experience, to the materiality of the "*world*", of the things making up the world, is also illuminated in Wallace Stevens's poems. Let us consider his less known poem *The American Sublime:*

How does one stand
To behold the sublime, to confront the mockers,
The mickey mockers
And plated pairs?

When General Jackson
Posed for his statue
He knew how one feels.
Shall a man go barefoot?
Blinking and blank?

But how does one feel?
One grows used to the weather,
The landscape and that;
And the sublime comes down
To the spirit itself,

The spirit and space,
The empty spirit
In vacant space.
What wine does one drink?
What bread does one eat?"
(Stevens 130-131).

As in the more famous *The Snow Man*, the tension of *The American Sublime* is developed by means of the poet's opposing the things of nature to human consciousness experiencing them. Unlike bursts of anxiety occasionally found in Emily Dickinson's poems, Stevens treats the opposition in a more distant, relaxed, scholarly way. The sublime knowledge is to be had at the expense of mocking everydayness, at the end of our doing away with the intentionality of consciousness, through our identification with the material otherness. Although "*the sublime comes down /to the spirit itself*", it is "*The empty spirit/In vacant space*".

Both poets' main concern was, however, to reach this knowledge most fully and directly. While Stevens was trying to do it through the extreme materiality of being, Dickinson went through the states of emotional and existential intensity. Whatever way, their art has placed them in the same camp – the one which is not concerned with ideological issues.

WORKS CITED

Dickinson, Emily."Shorter Poems." *The Norton Anthology of American Literature: Third Edition,*. Eds. Nina Baym et al. New York and London: W. W. Norton & Company, 1989. 1096-1120.

Freeman, Donald C. "Cognitive Metaphor and Literary Theory: Towards the New Philology." *Tracing Literary Postmodernism.* Ed. Tibor Žilka. Nitra: University of Constantine the Philosopher.71-84.

Gregory, Marshall. "*Style.*" 1998. [Cited on 26th June 2002; 08:40 CEST]. Available from WorldWideWeb: <http://www.findarticles.com/cf_0/m2342/2_32/54637191/p1/article.jhtml?term=Ethical+criticism%3A+what+it+is+and+why+it+matters>

Hartman, Geoffrey. *Criticism in the Wilderness: The Study of Literature Today*. New Haven and London: Yale University Press, 1980. 124.

Ogden, C. K.- Richards, I. A. *The Meaning of Meaning*. New York: Harcourt, Brace & World, Inc., 1946.

Perloff, Marjorie. "The Fascination of What's Difficult: Emily Dickinson and the Theory Canon." *Stand.* 2:2 (June 2000):31-32, (article on 31-49).

Scholes, Robert. *Semiotics and Interpretation*. New Haven and London: Yale University Press, 1982.

Sokal, Alan. "Transgressing the Boundaries: Toward a Transformative Hermeneutics of Quantum Gravity." *Social Text* 46.47. 217-252. [cited on 26th June 2002; 08:00 CEST]. Available from World Wide Web: <http://www.physics.nyu.edu/faculty/sokal/transgress_v2/transgress_v2_singlefile.html>

Stevens, Wallace: *The Collected Poems.* New York: Vintage Books, 1990.

PART II

POSTMODERN FICTION AND FILM

II.1 Cristina Garrigós: Multicultural Postmodernism: Ethics and Aesthetics

Multiculturalism and Postmodernism are two terms whose use has become widespread, especially in the past decades, although the relationship between them is quite ambiguous. In order to connect them, this paper will mainly address four questions, whose answers are by no means easy, much less generical, and are meant to open up a discussion rather than to offer definite answers.

1. Is multiculturalism a phenomenon characteristic of the postmodern age? (Is it something new or does it work differently in the postmodern age?)
2. How is the identity problem solved within the postmodern multicultural experience? (on the one hand, minorities reaffirming their essential identity, on the other hand, the postmodern questioning of this belief in the essence, proposing instead a constructed identity based on language)
3. Does multiculturalism presuppose a denial of the Western Rationalistic Tradition?

Or, in other words, do ethnic literatures attempt to subvert the "master" historical Western discourse?

4. Do contemporary ethnic narratives have anything in common with postmodernist (traditionally white and male) aesthetics? If so, what and why?

1. Is Multiculturalism a Postmodern Phenomenon?

To many minority critics and writers, Postmodernism is associated with Eurocentric views, especially due to its connection with Modernism, and with white-Anglo-writers. One had only to take any book on Postmodernism published in the 1970's or 1980's to see that the authors discussed were, in John Barth's words, "*the usual suspects*": Thomas

Pynchon, Robert Coover, William Gass, Edgar Lawrence Doctorow, John Barth himself, etc. No women, no "*ethnic*" writer.[1]

However, if we take the *The Norton Anthology of Postmodern American Fiction* (1998), we will see that things have changed, and the relationship between Postmodernism and Multiculturalism has become a strong one. A quick look at the table of contents will show that the authors included in this selection conform to a panoramic view of the different cultures that inhabit the US. Thus, to the canonical Postmodernist writers mentioned above such as Pynchon, Barthelme, Gass, Vonnegut, Barth or Coover, the new *Anthology* makes sure to include not only women (Jayne Ann Philips, Susan Daitch, Bobbie Ann Mason, or Joanna Russ) that were previously denied access to the "*club of postmodernist authors*" but also a representation of different minorities: Asian-American (Maxine Hong Kinston, Theresa Hak Kyung Cha), African-American (Notzake Shange, Ishmael Reed, Audre Lord, Toni Morrison), Chicanos + Latinos (Gloria Anzaldúa, Ricardo Cortez Cruz, Helena Maria Viramontes, Rosario Ferré) and Native American (Leslie Marmon Silko, Sherman Alexie, Gerald Vizenor)[2].

Such a wide variety of writers is a very good sample of the multicultural scene dominant in the United States nowadays. Moreover, the editors of the *Anthology*, Paula Geyh, Fred G. Leebron and Andrew Levy, in the short biographical note and information that introduce each writer make their ethnicity very explicit to call the attention of the readers to the very specificity of their gender and race. As the editors affirm in the introduction, the aesthetics of postmodernism seems especially appropriate for minorities' literature and this, in turn, has many interesting things to contribute to the postmodern debate (apparently still alive) because of their specificity, and so they say that *"the newfound heterogeneity of American Culture also manifests itself in postmodern*

[1] And I use the word "ethnic" aware of the problematics of its use and the fact that one way or the other we all belong to an ethnia.

narratives where authors have emphasized the complexities of identity and its embrace of hybrid forms and styles"(Leebron, Levy 1998: xiii).

For these editors, postmodernism and its distrust of the "official story" provides a very useful tool for the recognition of other voices and other stories:

"The retrospective bent of postmodern literature, as well as the dismantling of the myth of a unified narrative, of American history, has provided greater opportunities for the recognition of African-American (as well as American Indian, Chicano/a, Puerto Rican and Asian-American) versions of American history. Most significantly, the postmodern exploration of how power relations are encoded in language and how identity is culturally constructed, have been remarkable tools for comprehending racism in America" (xxviii).

In my opinion, what is interesting about this edition is the fact that even if attention is called to the race and culture of origin of the authors—ironically, when many of them would advocate the "death of the author"—these texts appear together, co-existing in a transethnic and transcultural way. They go beyond the very specificity of their ethnic group to interact with others in questions such as genre and aesthetics, to the extent that these editors have considered them worthy of the label "Postmodernist". Not Afro-American Postmodernism, Native-American Postmodernism, Latino Postmodernism or Asian American Postmodernism, but American Postmodernism.

2. The Identity Problem: Otherness

In her essay, *Postmodernism, Native American Literature and the Real: the Silko-Erdrich Controversy*, Susan Pérez Castillo has explored

---

[2] And one could include Jewish writers here such as Grace Paley, Walter Abish, Philip Roth, or E.L. Doctorow, although the situation of Jewish literature is somewhat different from that of the other minorities mentioned above.

the inner tension concerning the identity problem in postmodernist minorities' literature. In this article, Pérez Castillo points out the futility of Silko's acerbic critique of Erdrich's book, *The Beet Queen*, which she finds representing the author's negation of her "essential" identity to surrender to more fashionable "*academic, postmodern, so-called experimental influences*". For Silko (who is paradoxically also included in the *Norton Anthology of American Postmodern Fiction*), the postmodern literary aesthetics crashes completely with the Native-American oral tradition and implies the denial of any political conviction. Interestingly enough, Pérez Castillo manages to prove in her article not only that Silko's fiction is very close to the postmodernist aesthetics she despises, but also that Erdrich's narrative does not represent any treason to her origins by exposing the fragmentation of the experience, and rather enhances its political thrust by presenting ethnicity as a complex phenomenon rather than a simple, essentialist one. What I find particularly interesting in Pérez Castillo's essay is her denouncing of the limited position that an essentialist, logocentric perspective offers when dealing with ethnicity, a point where she fully agrees with Werner Sollors.

Almost twenty years ago, in an article titled *A Critique of Pure Pluralism* (1986), Werner Sollors was already criticizing the idea of culture as a mosaic. He was aware of the problems that a group-by-group approach may evoke: marginalization, racism, essentialism, etc. He proposed instead an *"openly transethnic procedure"* favoring connections between the groups and cultural interplay. Nevertheless, this is not to say that it is not important to be aware of the cultural specificities of a group to understand its claims, but not taking into account its connections with other groups in terms of a similar understanding of the literary act can, according to Sollors, provide us with a very partial, temporal and insufficient characterization.

Of course, one of the main problems when discussing pluralism or multiculturalism is the question of identity, which becomes even more complex in a postmodernist context. Postmodernism understands identity as a linguistic and cultural construction, distrusting the notion that identity is something grounded in nature, "essential". Obviously, this conception of identity collides with the reaffirmation of the "nature" of one's race, a belief that some cultures, for instance the African-American, are especially interested in defending and affirming the specificity of their culture on the grounds of nature. As in her essay *Postmodern Blackness* (1990) bell hooks writes:

"It never surprises me when black folks respond to the critique of essentialism, especially when it denies the validity of identity politics by saying 'Yeah, it's easy to give up identity, when you got one"(hooks 1998: 628).

According to Fredric Jameson, microgroups and "minorities" (where he includes women and "*the internal Third World*", as he calls it) often repudiate the idea of Postmodernism, associating it with a white and male-dominated group in power, an elite that can decenter easily their identity, since it is something well grounded and established. And yet, for Jameson,

"the micropolitics that correspond to the emergence of this whole range of small-group, non-class political practices is a profoundly postmodern phenomenon"(Jameson 1992: 318).

The reality of groups is, for him, related to the institutional collectivization of contemporary life, where the concept of "*groups*" becomes different to those of "*class*" and "*status*". Thus, in the postmodern society the dominant is:

"an ideology of groups, a set of phantasmic representations, that triangulate three fundamental pseudoconcepts: democracy, the media, and the market" (320).

The popular (and false) image of American democracy has defined the United States from its foundational constitution as the land where all persons, regardless of race, religion and gender are equal before the law. Such a credo has attracted people to come to the USA from all over the world in the belief that they would find a place of justice and equality there. And yet, many people think that although the contemporary postmodernist society emphasizes the plurality of ethnicities, cultures, genders, truths, realities and sexualities, with the idea that no particular type should be privileged over others, this celebration of the difference allows no space for difference itself, since all cultures and ideologies become subsumed in a global one. For some people, ethnic cultures are appropiated and commodified.[3] It is the belief of postmodernist detractors that by grouping all kinds of cultures and traditions in a single space, Postmodernism creates a simulacrum of multiculturalism in a phallacea of equal power and opportunities. In the words of Michael Berliner and Gary Hull,

> *"ethnic diversity is merely racism in a politically correct disguise[...]we're being urged to glorify race, which means we're being asked to institutionalize separatism*"(Berliner, Hull).

Both Berliner and Gull point out the fact that defining people by their race can only ultimately lead to separation and racism.[4] Along the same lines, Martin Fields says that while Postmodernism tries to enhance understanding of the diversity among people, it actually creates a new

[3] An interesting opinion to this effect is that of the editor of the on-line journal, *The Free Arab Voice*, 13 (2000) Ibrahim Alloush that points out the hypocresy of the US postmodernist society and its façade of multiculturalism while imposing its socio-economic and cultural domination over the Third World. This opinion is particularly relevant after the 11-S.

[4] "Diversity and Multiculturalism: the New Racism" http://multiculturalism.aynrand.org/diversity.html

tribalism.[5] Or as Gertrude Himmelfarb points out, postmodern multiculturalism has the

"Pernicious effect to demean and dehumanize the people who are the subjects of history. To pluralize and particularize history to the point where people have no history in common is to deny the common humanity of all people, whatever their sex, race, class, religion" (Himmelfarb 1994:154).

A critic like Mc Evilley reminds us that the adjective "*multi-culti*" has become a mocking term for the general intercultural tendency in the arts today (128). For him, Postmodernism, globalism and multiculturalism are synonyms (and so is post-colonialism) and they all represent a threat to the idea of quality, a reaction against formalism:

"Increasingly, it has become clear that in the emerging global scenario no one cultural group will be reinforced on all. Instead it will be one culture made of many cultures, one history made of many histories—a whole made of disunited fragments, with no imperative to unite them. People clinging to their own heritages, traditions, languages and styles of selfhood insists that they be written into history as themselves, and that their picture of us, with elements we might not relish, be written into that history too"(Mc Evilly 1999:132).

Those who were previously denied a voice in history want to speak now and provide their version of the story. But this version is necessarily partial, subjective and promotes their differentiality. If they were considered previously as "the other", now they privilege their otherness to articulate their discourse.

This emphasis on separatism is best represented by the hyphen that wants to bring the native ethnia close to the foster-mother nationality (African-American, Asian-American, Irish-American, etc.) with the

[5] "Postmodernism" *Premise*, vol. II, 8 (1995)

paradoxical result of the enhancing the separation of this specific group from the rest by foregrounding its essential identity and differential traits. On the other hand, as Isabella Furth has pointed out,

"the boom in the ethnic fiction market is the direct result of audiences' fetishitic desire to see the hyphen, to see it bare and authentic, bracketed and contained, thrown into the freak show prison of exoticism"(Furth in Miller 1995: 215).

We can thus say that the very term "*multiculturalism*" stresses the semi-autonomy of the different cultures, whereas terms like "*interculturality*" or "*transculturality*" stress instead the necessary interdependence among them, a dependence that is obviously formed by relations or tensions of domination and resistance: negotiations. These multicultural negotiations provide Postmodernism with something that was lacking and that was traditionally one of the main controversial points when discussing it: its political agenda. Although written by politically liberal authors, the fiction of writers like Barth, Coover, Pynchon, or Gass, was considered to be too abstract, too difficult to be understood by the common people and was thus classified as elitist and detached from reality.

Thus, much of the literature of the various cultures that live nowadays in the US combine the experimental fiction with the political message without being as elitist as their predecessor the Modernists or the white-male postmodern narrative of the 1960's and 1970's. This makes it very attractive for the literary market, so that, in a very postmodern way, the margins have been incorporated to the center, that is to say, the previously denied, or silenced, culture of the "*minorities*", the ex-centric (Hutcheon, 1988), has become the center, at least as far as popularity in academia is concerned.

3. Postmodernist Aesthetics and Multiculturalism

Hybridity of form and expression are frequently found in the fiction of ethnic writers: intertextuality, the opening out of history or the mix of genres, are narrative devices so frequently found in those texs that critics such as Celeste Olalquiaga observe that Latin American culture

"anticipate(s) postmodern pastiche and recycling, making the Third World Postmodern before the First World War" (Olalquiaga 1992).

Probably the reason why this critic says so is the use of the magic realist mode in much ethnic writing to such an extent that while some critics see magic realism as a particular strain of postmodernism (Hutcheon 1988; McHale 1992), others, like Theo D'haen, go one step further to affirm that *"the cutting edge of postmodernism is magic realism"*(201).[6] For D'haen, Magic realism is a way to have access to the main body of Western literatures for authors not sharing it, or not writing from a privileged position, and even do authors who come from the privileged center use it as a means to dissociate themselves from the discourse of power (D'haen 1995:195). Thus, magic realism implies decentering and also an implicit critique of the rationalist discourse.

The experimental writing practised by the minorities has an important ironic edge: being forced to use a foreign language, they try to detach themselves from it and from the Western literary tradition so as to offer a different perspective. Therefore, the use of non-conventional narrative devices is meant to allow the ex-centric discourses to speak and articulate their experiences of otherness. Thus, the postmodernist fiction of many ethnic writers is defined by a common preoccupation with emancipation from the privileged centers which they articulate by focusing on questions such as: history, domination, language, patriarchal control, memory, time, or, as I said before, otherness. This is evident in most

[6] There are several seminal essays on the relationship between Magical Realism and Postmodernism, such as Wendy B. Faris, "Scheherazade's Children: Magical Realism and Postmodern Fiction" and Theo D'haen "Magic Realism and

postmodernist minorities' texts. Let us consider these fragments from Sherman Alexie's *Captivity* included in *Postmodern American Fiction: A Norton Anthology* (1998):

1. "*When I tell you this story, remember it may change: the reservation recalls the white girl with no name or a name which refuses memory*" (342).
2. "*The best weapons are the stories and every time the story is told, something changes. Everytime the story is retold, something changes*"(343).
3. "*Language of the enemy: heavy lightness, house insurance, serious vanity, safe-deposit box, feather of lead, sandwich man, bright smoke, second-guess, sick health, shell game, still-walking sleep, forgiveness* "(343).

And compare them with Theresa Hak Kyung Cha's extracts from her *Dictee* included in the same anthology:

1. "*The 'enemy'. One's enemy. Enemy nation. Entire nation against the other entire nation. One people exulting the suffering institutionalized on another. The enemy becomes abstract. The relationship becomes abstract. The nation, the enemy, the name becomes larger thatn its own identiy. Larger than its own measure. Larger than its own signification*"(167-8).
2. "*There is no people without a nation, no people without ancestry*"(166)
3. "*She is born of one mother and a father*"(163).
4. "*Some will not know age. Some not age. Time stops. Time will stop for some. For them specially. Eternal time. No age. Time fixes for some. Their image, the memory of them is not given to deterioration, unlike the captured image that extracts from the soul precisely by reproducing, multiplying itself. Their countenance evokes not the*

Postmodernism: Decentering Privileged Centers" both in *Magical Realism. Theory, History, Community*. Lois Parkinson Zamora and Wendy B. Faris, eds.

hallowed beauty, beauty from the seasonal decay, evokes not the inevitable, not death, but the dy-ing"(170).

Or with Gloria Anzaldúa's texts from her *Borderlands/La Frontera:*

1. *"My 'stories' are acts encapsulated in time, 'enacted' every time they are spoken aloud or read silently. I like to think of them as performances and not as inert and "dead' objects (as the aesthetics of Western culture think of art works). Instead, the work has an identity; it is a 'who' or a 'what' and contains the presence of persons, that is, incarnations of gods or or natural and cosmic powers*"(185).
2. *"An image is a bridge between evoked emotion and conscious knowledge; words are the cables that hold up the bridge. Images are more direct, more immediate than words and closer to the unconscious. Picture language precedes thinking in words; the metaphorical mind precedes analytical consciousness*"(187).
3. "*I write the myths in me, the myths I am, the myths I want to become. The word, the image and the feeling have a palatable energy, a kind of power. Con imagénes domo mi miedo, cruzo los abismos que tengo por dentro. Con palabras me hago piedra, pájaro, puente de serpientes arrastrando a ras del suelo todo lo que say, todo lo que algún día seré"*(188).
4. *"When I write it feel like I'm carving bone. It feels like I'm creating my own face, my own heart— a Nahuatl concept. My soul makes itself through thc creative act. It is constantly remaking and giving birth to itself through my body. It is learning to live with la Coatlicue that transforms living in the Borderlands from a nightmare into a numinous experience. It is always a path/state to something else"*(190).

I am aware that I have made a selection of fragments from another selection of fragments: *The Norton Anthology*. We know that any selection is arbitrary and necessarily subjective and partial, but I wanted to group these fragments in order to point out the existence of more affinities than differences in the representation of linguistic and social estrangement (the language of the enemy), memory and its role in the recreation of the past (history) through the stories (literature). This becomes even clearer when it is embodied in the portrayal of women as victims of a patriarchal and hierarchical system: a martyr ("Yu Guan Soon") or a captive (Mary Rowlandson) propelled by internal tensions of oppositions (Anzaldúa's mestiza). I do think that these affinities deserve some attention and that a fact that the so-called ethnic literatures also want to be represented by postmodernist aesthetics does not imply a negation of their respective cultures but rather opens up new fields for study, expression, and communication.

WORKS CITED

Anzaldúa, Gloria. “Borderlands/La Frontera” Geyh, Paula, Leebron, Fred L., Levy, Andrew eds. *Postmodern American Fiction: A Norton Anthology*. New York: W.W.Norton&Company, 1998.183-191.

Berliner, M., Hull,G. “Diversity and Multiculturalism: the New Racism.”Available from

<http://www.freedom21santacruz.net/issues/Family-autonomy/breakwall/multi-cult.html

1998>(February 5, 2005)

Cha, Theresa Hak Kyung. “Dictee.” Geyh, Paula, Leebron, Fred L., Levy, Andrew eds. *Postmodern American Fiction: A Norton Anthology*. New York: W.W.Norton&Company: 1998.161-173.

D'haen, Theo. “Magic Realism and Postmodernism: Decentering Privileged Centers.” *Magical Realism. Theory, History, Community*. Faris, Wendy B. and Zamora, Lois Parkinson, eds. Duke UP, 1995.

Faris, Wendy B. and Zamora, Lois Parkinson, eds. *Magical Realism. Theory, History, Community*. Duke UP, 1995.

Geyh, Paula, Leebron, Fred L., Levy, Andrew eds. *Postmodern American Fiction: A Norton Anthology*. New York: W.W.Norton& Company, 1998.

Himmelfarb, Gertrude. *On Looking into the Abyss. Untimely Thoughts on Culture and Society*. New York: Alfred A. Knopf, 1994.

hooks, bell. “Postmodern Blackness”. Geyh, Paula, Leebron, Fred L., Levy, Andrew eds. *Postmodern American Fiction: A Norton Anthology*. New York: W.W.Norton&Company: 1998.624-630.

Hutcheon, Linda. *The Poetics of Postmodernism. History, Theory, Fiction*. London: Routledge, 1988.

---. *The Politics of Postmodernism*. London: Routledge, 1989.

Jameson, Fredric. *Postmodernism, or the Cultural Logic of Late Capitalism*. Duke UP, 1992.

McEvilly, Thomas. *Art and Otherness. Crisis in Cultural Identity*. New York: McPherson & Co. 1999.

McHale, Brian. *Constructing Postmodernism.* London & New York: Routledge, 1992.

Miller, Carol E. "Fictions and Ethnicities: Reading and Writing Identity in American Literatures." *Fiction and Ethnicity in North America. Problems of History, Genre and Assimilation.* Aitor Ibarrola, ed. Uncilla P, 1995. 209-225.

Olalquiaga, Celeste. *Megalopolis: Cultural Sensibilities.* Minneapolis: University of Minnesota Press, 1992.

Pérez Castillo, Susan. "Postmodernism, Native American Literature and the Real: The Silko-Erdrich Controversy." *The Massachussetts Review* 32:2 (1991): 285-294.

II. 2 Pi-hua Ni: Pen(is) in John Barth's Fiction: From Androcentric to Androgynous Narrative Paradigm

I'm not *all* male, he [Fenn] reminds her
[Susan], nor you all female. Just
mainly.
---John Barth, *Sabbatical*

1. Introduction

The scholarship on John Barth can be roughly categorized into four rubrics. The first one deals with existential issue in the form of *Bildungsroman*, and Barth's early novels such as *The Floating Opera*, *The End of the Road* and *The Sot-Weed Factor* fall under this heading. In the light of the intricate relationship between language, text, being and the construction of subjectivity, some scholars adopt a postmodern vantage point to analyze *Lost in the Funhouse* and accordingly subvert the traditional conception of the relationship between and among being, language and the text (the world). The second category of the Barthian scholarship focuses on how Barth appropriates and recycles biblical allusions, Greek myths and even American Indian myths to create multiple narratives in his postmodern fictive world. The polyphonic heterogeneous narratives, by contemporizing different spatial and temporal plains and socio-historical and cultural zones, produce constant dialogue for inter-illumination, reciprocal re-examination and mutual subversion. This postmodern phenomenon is aimed at questioning the canonic concepts of language, reality, historiography and hegemony, on the one hand, and giving voice, on the other hand, to the disempowered and marginalized cultures, discourses, ethnic groups, etc. *The Sot-Weed Factor*, *Lost in the Funhouse* and *Giles Goat-Boy* are the classics under this headline. The influence of the story-telling artistry of *The Thousand and One Nights* on Barth's development of an idiosyncratic narrative craftsmanship is the concern of the third category of the Barthian scholarship. *Chimera* is the very novel that catches the critic's eyes. The last group consists of the controversy, impact and inspiration that Barth's essays on postmodern aesthetics have provoked. Barth's *The Friday Book* and *Further Fridays*— collections of the novelist's essays, prefaces and interviews— are the main source for discussions and debates. Stan Fogel and Gordon Slethaug have observed in passing in *Understanding John Barth* that

"[u]ntil his later fiction, LETTERS, Sabbatical, and The Tidewater Tales, Barth does not fully develop any female characters"(42).

Aside from discussing Barth's failure to develop full and round female characters, I shall take a step further to make a critique of phallocentrism underlying Barth's early works and many Barthian scholars' criticisms. This paper accordingly aims to examine Barth's fictive corpus and address the shift, or more specifically, the rupture in Barth's narrative from an androcentric paradigm (in Barth's early fiction such as *The Floating Opera*, *The End of Road* and *Dunyazade*) to an androgynous one (Barth's later novel *Sabbatical: A Romance*). Feminist critique and postmodern concept of gender-crossing will be adopted first to analyze Barth's early patriarchal narrative paradigm and then to foreground and applaud the novelist's ultimate accomplishment in achieving an androgynous narrative— what Virginia Woolf promotes in *A Room of One's Own* as the writing of the greatest literary mind. The objective of this paper is, firstly, to present and then acclaim Barth's artistic achievement in creating a fluent floating narrative that crosses genders— as manifested in the co-authoring and co-creativity of the couple (Fenn and Susan) in *Sabbatical.* Secondly, this research is done in the hope that it will break a new opening to the Barthian scholarship and invite more discussion and understanding of Barth's difficult but extremely interesting and artistic fictive world.

2. Androcentric Narrative Paradigm in Barth's Early Fiction

With the publication of *Literature of Exhaustion* and *Literature of Replenishment*, John Barth has established himself as an eminent postmodern novelist. Yet, how shall we assess Barth's achievement when postmodernism, with its proclaimed objective to challenge the idea of center, canon, Self, authority, representation and grand narrative, has fallen under fierce attack launched by feminist critics? For example, in *The Discourse of Others: Feminists and Postmodernism,* Craig Owen argues that

"[t]he absence of discussions of sexual difference in writings about postmodernism, as well as the fact that few women have engaged in the modernism/postmodernism debate, suggest that postmodernism may be another masculine invention engineered to exclude women" (61).

That is to say, women remain marginalized as Other and represented as Object in the essentially patriarchal postmodern operation. Then, how does Barth write under the sway of this androcentric discourse? Does Barth's gender circumscribe his representation of women in his novels? An examination of Barth's portrait of women will answer these questions and, by extension, gauge his accomplishment as a genuine postmodern novelist.

Speaking of gender, as early as in 1949 Simone de Beauvoir writes that *"one is not born, but rather becomes, a woman"* (de Beauvoir 1989: 267). And the same goes for a man. Beauvoir's exposure of the fact that social and cultural constraints determine the construction of gender challenges the essentialist notion of man/woman dichotomy and the related sexual roles. Nevertheless, it is not until the 1980s that gender consciousness starts to raise such a question as to what extent gender informs and complicates both the writing and reading of texts. Gynocritics— a feminist project first advanced by Elaine Showalter in *Toward a Feminist Poetics* to construct a female framework for the evaluation of women's literature, to establish new modes based on the study of female experience rather than to adopt male models and theories— presumes that all writing by women is marked by their gender. Thus in *Introduction: The Rise of Gender, Speaking of Gender* Showalter asserts that

"women writers are not free to renounce or transcend their gender entirely" (Showalter 1989: 4).

Feminist critique of men's writing on the other hand illustrates that men writers likewise articulate their gendered experience and therefore men's writing, like women's, is also a gendered discourse. A new binary arises at this point as the foregoing presupposition seems to imply that men and women, unable to escape the cultural and social restraints on the formation of their gender, respectively inscribe their gendered experience in their writing and that there is accordingly an androcentric writing versus an gynocentric one. Yet, isn't there any case of gender crossing? Isn't change or rupture a possibility in the literary inscription of a man/woman writer's gender provided that gender is socio-culturally constructed and, therefore, can be deconstructed and reconstructed?

A postmodern feminist perspective adopted herein to examine and analyze Barth's *Sabbatical* aims to argue for the metamorphosis that has been inscribed in Barth's literary opus— a change that shows Barth's fiction has transformed from an androcentric narrative paradigm manifested in his early fiction into an androgynous one in his late novel *Sabbatical*. That is to suggest that Barth's first novels are fraught with patriarchal ideology albeit they are aesthetically renowned postmodern fiction. As an eminent postmodern novelist and, as Barth himself claims, an "amateur" theorist, Barth has produced novels of postmodern color and essays on this movement and its characteristics.[1] For instance, *The Floating Opera*, Barth's first novel, is generally taken as an existential novel dealing with Todd Andrew's obsession with his father's suicide and his own anxiety toward death.[2] Nevertheless, the novel proper never

---

[1] John Barth, "Postmodernism Visited: A Professional Novelist's Amateur Review, *Further Fridays* (Boston: Little, Brown and Company, 1995): 291-310.

[2] For details about the existential approach to the novel, please see Richard Schickel, "The Floating Opera," *Critique* 6.2 (1963):53-67; Thomas Le Chair, "John

wants of postmodern game in that Todd undertakes his existential quest in the form of writing and that Todd's tricky narrative game self-reflexively exposes the very structure and development of the novel *The Floating Opera* in which Todd himself is the protagonist-writer. However postmodern this novel may be, it is androcentric in its portrait of Jane Mack as an object of Todd's sexual fulfillment and as a pawn for Harrison Mack's sexual experiment. Whereas Todd is depicted as an intelligent man in*quiring* about the cosmos, Jane is portrayed as a dumb woman who, incapable of independent thinking, obediently follows Harrison's proposal of *ménage à trois*:

"'*He* [Harrison] *doesn't expect any payment,' Jane assures Todd after their first coitus initiated and insinuated by Harrison, 'I mean, I don't either. You mustn't feel obliged at all, Toddy. The thing is to not make much of it; it was just for the pleasure of it; that's all'*" (30).[3]

This binary portrait of man/woman as subject/object and mind/body also prevails throughout Barth's early fiction such as *The End of the Road, The Sot-Weed Factor, Lost in the Funhouse* and *Chimera.* Besides, manifest is the phallocentric metaphor of the pen— a quill with a fountain of ink inside— as penis in Todd's case. As Jeannine, the child of Todd's adultery with Jane, evidences his procreative power, his autobiographical notes betoken his creativity— literally, his ultimate accomplishment in the self-reflexive title novel *The Floating Opera* and, existentially, his decision to live on. That is, Todd's literary creativity conflates with his sexuality and procreation. At this point, Barth as a male writer seems unable to exempt himself from the social and cultural duress

---

Barth's 'The Floating Opera': Death and the Craft of Fiction," *Texas Studies in Literature and Language* 14 (1973):711-30; Charles B. Harris, "Todd Andrews, Ontological Insecurity, and 'The Floating Opera,' *Critique* 18.2(1976): 34-50; Thomas Carmichael, "John Barth and the Novajos: Time and Indeterminacy in 'The Floating Opera' and 'The End of the Road,' *Notes on Contemporary Literature* 15.3 (1983): 9-10. Of critical works on *The Floating Opera*, most focus on Todd Andrew's existential dilemma, few on the registry of Todd and Harrison's homosexuality in the form of *ménage à trois*, but none on Jane.

[3] John Barth, *The Floating Opera and The End of the Road* (N.Y.: Doubleday, 1988).

upon the construction of his gender as a man even if he is a postmodern novelist attempting to deconstruct many a literary norm and novelistic canon.

Barth's *The End of the Road* similarly exemplifies the dualism of man-mind versus woman-body in patriarchal ideology. Joe Morgan in the novel proper is depicted as an emblem of Reason, God, the Creating and Ordering force whereas his wife Rennie Morgan a token of Unreason. Jake Horner, a colleague of Joe's, is a moral nihilist. Adoring Joe's intellectual strength and eloquence, Rennie regards her husband as a role model and strives to follow his footsteps. To train Rennie to do intellectual argument and logical development, Joe becomes a Pygmalion in his attempt to mold Rennie into his idea of what he himself should be (Noland 1980:19). Suffice it to say that Joe the God is forging Rennie in his "perfect" image. But Joe's image as a symbol of perfection and reason is completely shattered when Rennie unexpectedly discovers another aspect of her husband. One night, Jake eggs Rennie on to peep on Joe so as to see if her husband is really what he presents himself to be. Rennie with strong faith in Joe insists that

"[r]eal people aren't any different when they're alone. No masks. What you see of them is authentic" (319).[4]

Instigated by Jake who retorts that nobody is authentic, Rennie looks in through the window on the sly and is dumbfounded to eyewitness her "ideal" husband, in lieu of reading and pondering on rational reckoning, masturbating and picking his nose at the same time. Disillusionment following her irrational infatuation for her husband drives Rennie to seek from Jake further solace, both mental and sexual. Having learned of Rennie's adultery, Joe first asks Rennie for a rationale and then forces her to continue her adulterous relationship with Jake until Rennie is able to provide a justifiable motive for her infidelity and thus abides by his philosophy of one certain motive for one specific act. Poor Rennie eventually gets impregnated and the pregnancy of uncertain siring brings

---

[4] John Barth, *The Floating Opera and The End of the Road* (N.Y.: Doubleday, 1988).

about a disaster to the *ménage à trois*. Unable to forgive Rennie's "groundless" adultery and, above all, her failure to transform herself into what he wishes her to be, Joe, the vengeful God, simply puts a shotgun in Rennie's hand and threatens her "*suicide or murder.*" Joe's injunction in the trio's showdown almost drives Rennie to commit suicide if Jake does not intervene. Finally, Rennie chooses illegal surgery and dies on the table when she is undergoing the illicit abortion arranged by Jake with the Black Doctor.[5] With this conclusion to the novel, we may interpret that Barth as the author-god declares death as the last judgment on and an exemplary punishment for women who aspire, in the first place, to intellectual power which traditionally is a prerogative for men and who refuse, secondly, to fulfill the child-bearing role which patriarchy demands of women.[6]

In like manner, scholarship on *The End of the Road* embodies the ideological working of patriarchy on the critics—male and female critics alike. Commenting on Rennie's tragic death in *The End of the Road*, Jac Tharpe expresses his idea in *John Barth: The Comic Sublimity of Paradox* in the following fashion:

"The crucial episode in ***The End of the Road*** *appears to be that in which Jake and Rennie secretly observe Joe alone, cavorting in front of the mirror, engaging in numerous uncharacteristic acts, and finally masturbating.* ***Rennie notes later that all the trouble began at the point. Barth seems to make insufficient use of the idea that Joe is after all a fraud, not to Jake, who expects nothing of anyone, but to***

[5] Etymologically, the name Rennie implies renaissance, "*rebirth.*" This connotation carries two significances. On the one hand, it points to Joe's willful "*remolding*" of Rennie and Rennie's own aspiration for an intellectual metamorphosis. On the other hand, Rennie's tragic death casts an ironic light on the prospect and surmise of a rebirth.

[6] Please note that Jane Mack in *The Floating Opera* is a counterpart of Rennie Morgan in *The End of the Road*. The husbands' practice of *ménage à trois* makes the wives respectively bear conceptions whose fatherhood cannot be specified. Jane gives birth to Jeannine and lives on with her husband; in marked contrast, Rennie dies when undergoing an abortion.

his wife, who is then ineffectually responsible for the rest of what happens in the novel. *Rennie, the person who has previously had neither a positive nor a negative approach to life, becomes the generating force in events because****, instead of following her husband's rationale further, she irrationally does what she wants to do****, as an older version of Jeannine, the child in* **the Floating Opera** (Tharpe 1974: 31, emphasis added).

The above comment reflects the male critic's sexist concept. First, all the trouble in Joe and Rennie's marriage begins as early as the time when they are just boy and girl friends, and Rennie has been at Joe's mercy, suffering from his physical and spiritual abuse. The peeping scene is the point for disillusionment and thus a surfacing of the subterranean trouble in their marriage. It is unbelievable to see any critic suggesting that Rennie should accept perverse suggestions and cold rationales from her heartless husband. What suggestions has Joe given Rennie? Pushing Rennie to Jake's room to test how strong her will is and driving her to keep adulterous relationship with Jake until she can come up with a proper rationale for her "*betrayal*"! What predicament and ruin has Joe created for Rennie after she has followed like a pious disciple Joe's "*divine*" orders? An unwelcome and sorrow-inflicting pregnancy of confusing parentage! And what does Joe react to her pregnancy? A chilly gesture of putting a gun in Rennie's hand and a bloody suggestion that she take her own life! All are ridiculous proposals and spiritual abuse save a good rationale. As a human being, Rennie has the autonomy on her own body and life. Her decision on abortion is the first significant breakthrough in her marriage, her first assertion of her right. Rennie's tragedy results not from her self-assertion but from having listened to men (Joe and Jake). Nothing but androcentrism can explain the fact that Tharpe, as a male critic, also singles out Rennie to blame for her death when Barth does not allow Rennie to survive and mature after her awakening.

Charles B. Harris asserts likewise in *Passionate Virtuosity* that Rennie represents the body and, led by his patriarchal chauvinistic view, he argues that Rennie's own physicality holds responsibility for her tragedy:

"Despite ***the calculated efforts*** *of Jake and Joe, Rennie conceives"* (43, emphasis added). Harris' effort to whitewash and legitimate Joe and Jake's collaborative masculine violence and sin proves that Harris either ignores or does not care how much Rennie is manipulated and exploited, both physically and emotionally, by both men in their masculine contending game of rational power. Like the Barth of the time when he wrote the novel proper, Harris' critical review reflects a phallocentric (sub)consciousness.

And some female critics also embrace the androcentric vintage point in their analyses of Barth's characterization of Rennie. Explaining the diminished and victim role of Rennie in *The End of the Road*, Patricia Tobin, for instance, follows Barth's lead in his 1968 interview that the two-men-and-one-woman *ménage à trois* aims to make male characters embody ideas (thesis and antithesis alike) whereas female character serve as catalyst or object for the two men's intellectual contestation:

"A probable reason for the recurrence in my stories of the triangle, that takes the form of one woman and two men instead of the other around, is that if you have for thematic reasons a character who represents single-mindedly some position, then the dictates of drama suggest that you're likely to have another character who's his antithesis—these are likely to be male characters if they're embodiments of ideas—then you need a woman between to be the catalyst for the reaction between the two males so that you can work out your dialectic"(Prince 1968, 46)(qtd. in *John Barth and the Anxiety of Continuance* 44).[7]

This statement made by the young Barth in his early interview speaks of a patriarchal conceptualization of man/woman as subject/ object and attests to the novelist's gender construction.

---

[7] Patricia Tobin, *John Barth and the Anxiety of Continuance* (Philadelphia: U of Pennsylvania P, 1992).

Patriarchy has long instituted the ideology that man goes for intellectual reasoning and confrontation while woman for submission and obedience and that man born with critical faculty acts as the subject whereas woman susceptible to sentiment and whim is the object. That Joe and Jake embody and fight for conflicting abstract ideas and philosophical positions at the expense of Rennie, who, in her desperate yearning to imitate her husband and thus to become a rationalist, submits to Joe's wills to allow herself a mistress of Jake, gives full expression to the typical sexist and patriarchal conception about the male/female, reason/whims and subject/object dichotomy constituting the young Barth's mentality and (sub)consciousness. Tobin's endorsement for the diminutive characterization and weight Barth gives to Rennie and her remark on the tragic coda Barth puts to the novel proper that *"the woman [Rennie] drops out, **an object** that has served its purpose of bringing together two men in conflictual violence and mimetic identification"* (45 emphasis added) illustrates that the woman critic is embroiled with masculine chauvinism.

In a similar vein, androcentrism finds its expression in *Dunyazadiad.* Structured as a framed story of a triad, *Dunyazadiad* in *Chimera* is typical of Barth's postmodern textual game. However, the novella still demonstrates a patriarchal narrative paradigm at two points. First of all, disguising himself as the Genie conversing in Dunyazade's story with Scheherazade on the parallel relationship between writing (story-telling) and love-making, Barth remarks that *"[n]arrative, in short, was a love relation*" and

"[t]he teller's role[...] regardless of his actual gender, was essentially masculine, the listener's or reader's feminine, and the tale was the medium of their intercourse"(34).[8]

---

[8] A description about what the Genie looks like and what life he has led points straight to John Barth himself. Following this self-portrait, we can tell for sure that the Genie is a surrogate of and a mouthpiece for Barth. In addition, "genie" means "genius" in German. See John Barth, "Dunyazadiad," *Chimera*, (N.Y.: Fawcett Crest, 1972)16;20. Further citations from the text are of the same edition and will be indicated with page number in parentheses.

This notion of writing (story-telling) as a masculine activity originates from Western phallocentrism. In *Creativity and the Childbirth Metaphor: Gender Difference in Literary Discourse*, Susan Stanford Friedman explains the source of this sexually biased ideology:

*"Words about the production of babies and books abound with puns, common etymologies, and echoing sounds that simultaneously yoke and separate creativity and procreativity. This wordplay reveals not only currents of unconscious thought as Sigmund Freud has described but also the structures of patriarchy that have divided **labor** into men's **production** and women's **reproduction**. Underlying these words is the familiar dualism of mind and body, a key component of Western patriarchal ideology. **Creation** is the act of the mind that brings something new into existence. **Procreation** is the act of the body that reproduces the species. A man conceives an idea in his brain, while a woman conceives a baby in her womb, a difference highlighted by the post-industrial designation of the public sphere as man's domain and the private sphere as woman's place. The **pregnant** body is necessarily female; the **pregnant** mind is the mental province of genius, most frequently understood to be inherently masculine"*(75)[9]

Therefore, the aforementioned assertion of the Genie Barth foregrounds the articulation of Barth's gender and of his mental assimilation of phallocentrism.

In her story to her husband Shah Zaman (i.e. Part I, the innermost narrative frame, of *Dunyazadiad*), Dunyazade narrates how her sister Scheherazade has instructed her to take revenge for their sex in general and for the women put to death by King Shahryar and his brother Shah Zaman the very first morning after the royal siblings' wedding night:

"[T]he patriarchy isn't changed," says Scheherazade, "I believe it will persist even to our Genie's time and place"(45).

---

[9] See also Susan Stanford Friedman's elaboration on the Christian religious resonance of the childbirth metaphor that solidifies the separation of male creativity from female reproduction in "Creativity and the Childbirth Metaphor: Gender

Murdering the Sultan and his royal sibling, representative of patriarchy, symbolizes a subversion of the male power and dominance. This murder consciousness in Dunyazade's story is then to be realized in "reality" on the wedding night for Dunyazade and Shah Zaman and Scheherazade and King Shahryar (Part II, the second outer narrative frame, of *Dunyazadiad*). After finishing her story, Dunyazade shows Shah Zaman the razor for castration, symbolically for the demise of the disparity between the sexes. But, the Genie Barth as the *arche*narrator of this frame-story, brushes off the climax and eases the tension merely with greetings of warm "*good mornings*" not only between Dunyazade and Shah Zaman, Scheherazade and King Shahryar but by extension between the two sexes:

"The royal couples— Shahryar and Scheherazade, Shah Zaman and Dunyazade— emerge from their bridal chambers after the wedding night, greet one another with warm good mornings," narrates the Genie (63-64)".

Besides, the surrogate Barth concludes the novella as follows:

If I could invent a story as beautiful, it should be about little Dunyazade and her bridegroom, who pass a thousand nights in one dark night and in the morning embrace each other; they make love side by side, their faces close, and go out to greet sister and brother in the forenoon of a new life. Dunyazade's story begins in the middle; in the middle of my own, I can't conclude it— but it must end in the night that all good mornings come to[. . .] And no man knows it better than Shah Zaman, to whom therefore the second half of his life will be sweeter than the first"(64).

The Genie Barth's avowed conceit of *Dunyazadiad* covers up the imminent death threat the female have suffered and informs us of Barth's phallocentric psyche.

Expounding her murder scheme to Dunyazade, Scheherazade once remarks that

---

Difference in Literary Discourse," *Speaking of Gender*, intro. & ed. Elaine Showalter, (N.Y.: Routledge, 1989): 76.

"[t]hanks to Allah you can't be snared as I was in the trap of novelty, and think to win some victory for our sex by diverting our persecutors with naughty stunts and stories" (45).

Scheherazade's comfort derives from the would-be *groom*cide, regicide and the prospective liberation from masculine tyranny and violence. Unlike Scheherazade who, for years, has painstakingly won her life one more day with one intriguing tale, Dunyazade is seemingly to escape Scheherazade's fate. Nevertheless, Dunyazade is the very tale-teller in the first narrative frame about Scheherazade and King Shahryar. In turn, Dunyazade is a creation out of the Genie Barth (the narrator of Part III and the outermost narrative frame of "Dunyazadiad") and Barth the author (the mastermind of the whole story). Dunyazade is therefore as entrapped as Scheherazade is by man's quill. Both of them are *the told* rather than *the teller* in Barth's fiction. This hard fact undercuts the strength of Barth's own claim in his interview with Charlie Reilly that *Dunyazadiad* is his first story told in woman's voice (15). Besides, my foregoing suggestion inevitably enters a critical dialogue with Harris's argument in *Passionate Virtuosity: The Fiction of John Barth.* On the teller/auditor relationship of the male and female characters in *Dunyazadiad*, Harris asserts that Scheherazade and Sharyahr, Dunyazade and Zaman, and the Genie take turns playing the roles of the teller and the listener and that they accordingly break down the gender boundary and constitute an androgynous whirl (Harris 1983: 131). However, the fact that the male Genie functions as the ultimate narrator of the three-layered narrative *Dunyazadiad,* nullifies without substantial justification women's resentment and baffles the female's revolt against patriarchy (exemplified by Scheherazade and Dunyazade) undermines Harris's thesis on an androgynous synthesis in *Dunyazadiad.* The Genie/man possesses the pen after all and, accordingly, gives the last word.

On the issue of narrative genders in *Dunyazadiad,* Gabriella Beditti's essay *Women's Sense of the Ludicrous in John Barth's 'Dunyazadiad'* also contributes to a fuller understanding of the complex threefold narrative and the recurrent shift in the narrative genders of the story proper. The Genie in the first narrative frame plays his role of masculine teller and Scheherazade the feminine auditor given the Genie-Barth's association of storytelling with gender relationship— that the storyteller is equivalent to the masculine role whereas the listener the feminine one. But, Beditti points out varied reversals in the addresser/addressee and masculine/feminine parallel. Scheherazade displaces the Genie as the masculine tale-teller because the stories the Genie tells are drawn from *The Thousand and One Nights* and by extension from Scheherazade. Thus, Scheherazade the audience becomes the yarn-maker whereas the Genie the storyteller the told. A similar inversion occurs in the second narrative frame, too. Keeping a sharp knife at Shah Zaman's genital for dismemberment, Dunyazade makes Shah Zaman listen to her story of women's grudge against male dominion and therefore the former obtains the masculine role of the teller while the latter the feminine role of the auditor. To foil Dunyazade's castration attempt, Shah Zaman makes up a story to justify the virgin-a-night policy that he and his royal brother King Shahryar have been practicing. The act of telling Dunyazade the story about their unilateral fidelity and the female treachery turns upside down the teller/told as masculine/feminine relationship and Dunyazade is in turn rendered the feminine audience. The eventual tale-teller and thus the masculine role is assigned to the Genie since the real narrator, the ultimate voice we have been hearing all along is that of the Genie— the host storyteller of the uttermost narrative frame.

Suggestive is Beditti's demarcation of the narrative genders in *Dunyazadiad;* arguable however is the critic's analysis of the characters' sexual roles and gender relationship in the story. Arguing against the belief that male humor is a defense mechanism bound in a tradition that upholds and prides the importance of control and female humor is a defense mechanism deriving from a tradition of self-effacing and belittlement, Bedetti asserts that Barth has rendered his Scheherazade with a peculiar sense of humor which enables her to perceive the ludicrous in the patriarchal notion of masculinity and breaks down the cycle of masculine power and feminine resistance generated by the opposition of male and female humor:

"Confronting Shahryar with pure irony would incur the charge of insolence and discourage change, while obsequiousness would merely enforce the status quo. The sisters are taking the middle ground by striking a ludicrous pose" (Bedetti 1985: 78).

King Shahryar, suggests Bedetti, has long desired to abolish his virgin-a-night vow but dare not do so lest his younger brother Shah Zaman would deem him chickenhearted. Discerning the ridiculousness and contradiction in her royal husband's yearning and hesitation, Scheherazade presents herself as the needed excuse to save the king's face and pleads for her life on behalf of their children rather than of her stories or herself. Bedetti therefore concludes that the royal brothers eventually accept equality between the sexes given that the "wise" Scheherazade maintains with her humor Shahryar's sense of maleness and his position as a custodian of truth whereas she, in fact, controls the situation and performs *"a secret gynocracy"* (80). Yet, Bedetti's foregoing assertion contradicts Virginia Woolf's pointed and insightful diagnosis in *A Room of One's Own* of the male superiority and psyche that

"[w]omen have served all these centuries as looking-glasses possessing the magic and delicious power of reflecting the figure of man at twice its natural size"

and consequently prevents me from coming to full agreement with the critic's inference about sexual equity (Woolf 1945:37). In spite of seeming rebellion, Barth's Scheherazade and Dunyazade have in fact played the role of the sweet angel of the house, always saying "*yes*" and "*as it pleases thee*" to their chauvinistic men, and, as a consequence, have fostered male domination and, worse, a pretension of male superiority. Provided this fact, I would contend, pace Bedetti, that Barth's "Dunyazadiad" projects a patriarchal value pattern rather than asserts equal footing for the two sexes.

Based on the examples and illustrations in this section, it can be argued that Barth's early fiction constitutes an androcentric narrative paradigm. My thesis herein finds strong support in one sense from Cynthia Davis' insightful paper *Heroes, Earth Mothers and Muses: Gender Identity in Barth's Fiction*— the only critical work that I know of which has made a feminist critique of Barth's early novels. In the essay, Davis charges that Barth's antifeminism has broached in his early fiction like *The Floating Opera*, *The End of the Road*, *The Sot-Weed Factor* and *The Giles Goat-Boy* and then becomes manifest bluntly in *Chimera*. Barth's literary works have always employed male-female relationship to explore questions of identity. But Barth's chauvinistic characterizations have escaped criticism, argues Davis, because his fictive opus, gradually turning from realism to parodic and self-conscious approach, allows him on the one hand to explore the traditional and archetypal structures (i.e. myths) at the heart of fiction, of experience and of perception, and on the other hand to camouflage his sexism with the disguise of a "new" myth. Therefore, an unmasking of the novelist's patriarchal ideology becomes an urgent task; otherwise, the masked phallocentrism will prove *"more deadening to women"* (Davis 1980: 309). In Barth's first two novels, Jane in *The Floating Opera* and Rennie in *The End of the Road* are portrayed as vegetative, empty, and shapeless people that count on their male counterparts for fulfillment and definition. *Menáge à trois* or triangle rivalry of two men for one woman makes the woman become a potential proving-ground for the man:

"The woman is desired less for herself than as a means of self-assertion and triumph over the rival" (310).

Women in Barth's portrait are like soft wax subject to men's free plying. In Davis' words,

"Barth attributes no energetic will to woman, no identity that she can choose as a man does, no completed sense of self; but he gives her the power of inertia, of being preceding definition. She is the blank reality that must be given a human face— a man's"(Davis 1980: 313).

In appearance, Barth's *Dunyazadiad* seems to testify the novelist's change in presenting more varied and developed women characters. Davis' analysis of the novella sheds light on the illusive nature of this presumption. The feminist critic argues that Scheherazade's tales are given by the Genie whereas Dunyazade's narrative power is conditioned by Shah Zaman and overwritten by the surrogate Barth. Based on the Genie Barth's formula of gender identity that the teller's role is masculine, the listener feminine and the tale the medium of their intercourse, both Scheherazade and Dunyazade are ***emasculated*** rather than empowered by men—both the male characters (the Shah Zaman and the Genie) and the male author (Barth). As for the other two novellas, two types of women are characterized. One is the devoted worshipper of the man; the other as a Muse. The former gives admiration to man but her dependence on him turns out to be a burden; the latter on the other hand encourages man for heroic quest and seems to function as man's fountain of inspiration and vitality. The second category presents a seemingly positive portrayal of woman's independence and activity. However, it is not the case, argues Davis,

"Any power the Muse has, then, is a catalyst or vehicle for the hero's imagination, not as independent element" (318).

That is to say, Barth makes a full circle in creating first the binary of male/female as subject/object and definer/defined and then lapsing toward a male-oriented structure by denying not only a balance between the opposing masculine and feminine qualities but also depriving his female characters even the traditional power of the feminine qualities such as that presented by Earth Mother. Therefore, unattainable in Barth's fiction is a genuine resolution and balance of the masculine and feminine qualities (the opposing poles) enacted in Woolf's character of Lily Briscoe, asserts Davis. Thus, Davis concludes:

"Such is Barth's interweaving of myth and aesthetic that it is hard to tell whether he uses the pattern without clearly seeing its implications or actually attacks feminism by what he thinks are its spokesmen[...]Barth's obsession with point of view holds the key: he accepts a male-oriented

mythic structure, in which the male is human, the female everything else. He does not question those assumptions in the way that he questions others, but accepts a symbolic identification as literally true"(320).

This conclusion sounds very hopeless about Barth's androcentric ideology and its projections in the novelist's fiction. But a probing into Barth's *Sabbatical* shall prove the opposite. There is no telling if it is Barth's response to the feminist's accusation of his sexism and antifeminism; nevertheless, there is no denial of such a rupture. The following section shall focus on the rupture that occurs in Barth's latter novel *Sabbatical*.

3. Androgynous Narrative Paradigm in Barth's *Sabbatical*

Sabbatical is a story talking-writing about Fenn and Susan talking-writing a story about their talking-writing about their joint writing and mutual loving. In a sense, Barth continues his postmodern frame story that he has employed since his early novels and short stories. What is special about *Sabbatical* lies in the fact that the narrative is not only about Fenn and Susan— that is, a story *about them*, but also *done together* by Susan and Fenn— that is, a story *of theirs*. Provided this peculiarity, I dub *Sabbatical* an ***androgynous postmodern narrative*** and evaluate it as a metamorphosis in Barth's novelistic virtuosity— a shift from an androcentric to an androgynous narrative paradigm. This assertion will be justified as follows.

Thematically, Barth's *Sabbatical* is a narrative dealing with a double quest: It is a quest, on the one hand, to search for Susan's missing half-brother Gus, who supports the socialist government of the late President Salvador Allende Gossens, which CIA wants to "*destabilize,*" and Fenn's disappeared twin brother and Gus' father, Manfred, who works for CIA. On the other hand, the sailing adventure is a quest to re-examine Susan and Fenn's past and present life and to find an outlet and opening for their future:

"It was our hope and intention that by the end of this same voyage we would know better our hearts and minds vis-à-vis several decisions which lie ahead; but by and large we don't, yet" (83-84).[10]

On their sabbatical, they are faced with indecisiveness about their career. As Fenn and Susan profess, *"We speak desultorily, as if waiting for the plot of our lives to get on with it"* (235). The couple's floating life— on sea or on land— is not unlike a man at a crossroad. That is, the hero and heroine are *"at a Y," "at a fork in the road"* (236; 284). Simultaneously, a narrative crisis parallels their life crux. Fenn and Susan are tackling off the knot in their literary effort to give birth to a story, as they are struggling with the trial in their life. The couple are collaborating to give form to the narrative on their life story just as they are striving together to *create* order/goal for their life:

"If literally we don't know where we're going from Gibson Island and Baltimore, it's because figuratively we don't know where we are" (236).

Therefore, overcoming their block in writing means conquering the trial for their life, and vice versa. Decision must be made so as to have confluence after divergence. Fenn and Susan cannot solve their problem, both in life and in creative labor, until they finally make the decision that they will begin where they end— that is, they will keep sailing and their story will keep going (366). In so doing, they eventually push through the bottleneck both in their life and narrative.

To prove Barth's androgynous narrative in *Sabbatical*, my analysis will first of all address the novelist's characterization of Susan. Subverting his own earlier convention and the patriarchal literary tradition, Barth characterizes Susan as a professional, critical, creative and talented woman. Susan's comment on Byron's *Manfred* and Manfred's incestuous relationship with Astarte attests to this aesthetic rupture in Barth's novelistic representation of women. Since full and adequate characterization of women characters is rare in Barth's fiction, Barth's

---

[10] John Barth, *Sabbatical: A Romance* (Normal: Dalkey Archive Press, 1996). Subsequent citations from the text are of the same edition and shall be indicated with page number in parentheses

portrayal of Susan as a woman capable of both emotion and intelligence is exceptional. The tradition of literary female image always associates women with body, baby breeding, child rearing, passivity, whim, emotion and sentiment, and denies women the competence of intelligence, critical independent thinking, will and creativity. Women are eventually deprived of voice. In *Sabbatical*, Barth breaks away from this patriarchal convention and creates an intelligent woman who holds a doctoral degree, working as an associate professor of American literature and creative writing. More importantly, Susan demonstrates her literary creativity in the writing of *Sabbatical*, which is metafictionally a brainchild out of Susan and Fenn's co-authoring and co-creativity (12-14).

In her dialogue with Fenn on diction and narrative technique, Susan observes that

"a certain range and variety of diction— not only as between the speech of various characters in a story, to help differentiate and characterize them [Aristotle's aesthetic idea in Poetics], but also within the prevailing narrative voice itself—can be both refreshing and strategic: a change of rhetorical pace; a humanizing shift of perspective"(12).[11]

The narrative pattern of the following quote (a mode which I term as **spoused narrative**) prevails throughout *Sabbatical*; and ***the flowing narrative*** in/of the novel is, in fact, a realization of Susan's aesthetic idea on the change of perspective:

"I get to see my new man's competence, if not grace, under pressure. His patience, reasonableness, and high flapping-point. His knowledgeability and range of experience, compared to mine. His knack for making almost anything work. His unaffectedness and general amiability. His good humor and spaciousness of heart. Plus, frequently, his penis.

I get to see my new woman's logistical good sense; her cheerfulness in adverse circumstances; her culinary resourcefulness and skill; the way she learns things fast and doesn't forget them; her enjoyment of all kinds of people and situations, and her canny assessment of them; her general pluckiness— I'd even say courage. Her spaciousness of heart. The number and variety of her passions. And lots of her skin"(196).

Fenn and Susan as narrative partners take turns expressing each's view of the other and create with their joint force a fluent coupled narrative. Moreover, the subtle and fluent shift from one narrative viewpoint to another also gives force to Barth's generation of a flowing androgynous narrative in *Sabbatical*. Here is an instance:

"As Fenn pauses at the boarding ladder to toss the ball into the cockpit, we are startled by lewd catcalls from among the trees on the high bank: Wash 'em off, baby! Float it over here! Et cetera. The voice is male, mocking, loud as if amplified. Susan swirls around, alarmed; sees no one but Fenn, in the opposite direction; strikes out for the boat. Lewd whistles follow her. Dig that ass!"(48)

This part of the narrative begins with Susan/third-person singular viewpoint, glides into the first-person plural *we* and then shifts to Fenn/third-person singular viewpoint. This flowing of narrative perspective— from individual (male and female) to joint one— illustrates symbolically the collaborative and intertwining nature of an androgynous narrative.

Another narrative type to demonstrate Fenn and Susan's co-authoring is **the 50-to-50 narrative relay**. In the midst of her flashback narrative about their respective family backgrounds and how they meet and get married, Susan asks Fenn to take over the narrative: *"Would you take it for a while, Fenn? Fleshing beck wears a girl out"* (179).[12] This mode of androgynous narrative envisions a scene in which two narrators relay their cooperative story-making. Of course, Barth never forgets to varify the narrative— or precisely speaking, to create divergence so as to create convergence. At Susan's request, Fenn takes over the narrative. Nevertheless, he deviates to give an account on CHOTTANK SAFE-

[11] Bracketed information added for comparison and italics mine for emphasis.

[12] Susan shows her literary strength through such wordplays as "fleshbeck" and flashback, "flesh out" and "flush out," etc. Besides, Susan calls her husband Fenn

HOUSE STORY— a narrative about his past career as a CIA operative for the clandestine division Company and how he, his twin brother Manfred and other agents (esp. future DINA people) torture men who are anti-American or who have American interests at stake. Only after he has finished his burst on the CIA intelligence and its torture business does Fenn return to pick up Susan's story on their past. It is at this point that Fenn returns from a divergence to form a convergence in their narrative (183).

The fourth narrative type, named **the merged narrative**, is the subtlest one in Barth's design of the couple's story telling. Fenn and Susan take turns narrating their story about their unexpected ante-marital encounter on sea. Barth keeps the same first-person singular "I" and first-person plural "we" narrative voices and, accordingly, creates a smooth flow of narrative collaboratively done by the couple. To demonstrate this point, it is necessary to quote a fairly extensive section:

"Three miles wide there, I believe. There's a northerly blowing; the first leg is a run, but then the river U-turns, and we're beating up against wind and tide. How about you? Our canoe trip hasn't worked out, and the week we've allowed for it is nearly up. We've left my car in Chestertown and started on the upper river, but the tidal current up there runs more strongly than I expected, and that week it's in the wrong direction from midmorning to midafternoon. So we've come downstream instead, where the river's wider and thecurrent's less strong[...]Late afternoon. Cacaway's our destination for the day. I'm hoping the wind will blow out overnight, so Mim and I can head up toward Chestertown in the morning. When I see this sailboat beating in our direction against the chop, I know we'd be swamped out there in open water. I'm also hoping you'll anchor behind Cacaway, whoever you are, so we can scrounge some ice[Susan's narrative]. But I've just decided that the wind is northeast enough for us to keep sailing if we take the West Fork, whereas we'd have to power into it up the East Fork. We've spotted a canoe—the only other boat in sight—

"Fensie" so as to pun on the word "*fancy*" and thus conveys the message that Fenn can read her mind.

and as we come about, Orrin checks with the binocs to see whether its occupants are signaling for help. He reports that it's two chicks shirtsailing. Topless?[Fenn's narrtive] We have our life vests on. [Susan's narrative][...] We meet. Oroonoko gets the sails down; I start up the diesel; we chug over to see whether we can help. He checks with the glasses and says They're okay; they're swimming their canoe toward the island; they seem to know what they're doing. Then he says Hey Dad, for Christ's sake, it's Susan! It's Suse and Miriam! [Fenn's narrative]Full speed ahead, to the good part. We don't need help getting ashore, but I'm plenty relieved to see Uncle Fenn and Cousin Orrin, as well as happily surprised. I've hardly heard that you've bought a boat, much less that you're cruising in the neighborhood. I guess our two families are less in touch in these than we've ever been. Have you dropped anchor?[Susan's narrative]We've seen that you're in no danger; but a swamped canoe isn't easy to swim to shore with in a chop, and all your gear is wet[...] [Fenn's narrative]"(184-87)[13]

On Barth's innovation exemplified in the above quoted passage, Zack Bowen mistakenly complains in *A Reader's Guide to John Barth* about its "inconsistent" narrative viewpoint and attributes this fault to Fenn as a novice like Ambrose in *Lost in the Funhouse*:

"Fenn does know a lot about sailing, but a lot less about standard novel-writing techniques: His narrative point of view is inconsistent, moving between first-person singular and plural, as well as third-person and third omniscient voices intermittently speaking along with authorial digressions and a long series of excerpts from Baltimore and Wilmington newspapers on the John Arthur Paisley story[. . .]All these seeming narrative infelicities resemble the amateurish remarks of the youthful narrator of such pervious Barth tales as 'Lost in the Funhouse' and describe realistically the process engaged in by novices in their initial attempt at fiction"(107).

[13] Bracketed information added for clarification. Susan calls her husband Fenn uncle because her mother Carmen marries Manfred, Fenn's brother.

Likewise, in *Floating Signifiers in John Barth's Sabbatical* Gordon E. Slethaug writes that

"[t]he indeterminate, discontinuous rotation of narrators creates a precarious narrative with equivocal readings"(Slethaug 1987: 651).

But the high point of which these critics remain oblivious is that the constant shifts in narrative vantage point can be interpreted as Barth's utterance of the joint male-female collaboration (i.e. Fenn and Susan's) in creating the novel *Sabbatical*.

In addition to these four narrative types that Barth employs to create Fenn and Susan's joint androgynous narrative, the novelist also appropriates the childbirth metaphor to inscribe the crisis and breakthrough both in the couple's life and literary endeavor. Their marital crisis climaxes with Susan's abortion and the subsequent divorce proposal. Susan has longed to have a kid. This yearning is implied in Susan's half-kidding wish that she would like to have a dynamite clandestine adulterous passionate affair and to have children named Andrew and Alexis. Susan and Fenn have once imagined that they would name their twin children Andrew and Alexis, for twins of a boy and a girl embody the ideal of androgyny. And Susan does bear twins of a boy and a girl, but she has the twins aborted for the sake of Fenn's heart problem. As long as Fenn does not want to have any child, Susan will not keep any:

"I could stand not having kids if it was me by myself, but I can't stand our not having them" (347).

Susan only welcomes the children who are welcome by both Fenn and her— that is, offspring of their physical consummation, spiritual union and emotional consensus. Therefore, Susan decides on abortion first without notifying Fenn of her pregnancy and informs him later of her choice.[14] However, Susan and Fenn complete their androgynous narrative

[14] The reader may note the contrast in Barth's portraits of Rennie in *The End of the Road* and Susan in *Sabbatical*. The former chooses and then dies of abortion

and give birth to the novel *Sabbatical*. Unlike her foremothers, Susan forsakes the traditional childbearing role for women and takes on an intelligent, intellectual and creative part— writing. Creative production substitutes physical reproduction.

But the genesis of a story does not come without pain and labor. Susan suffers an emotional outburst and breakdown after she has undergone the abortion. Initially, Fenn fails with his suggestion of a brainchild to assuage Susan's emotional turmoil; a deadlock in their literary creativity accordingly follows the crisis as a result of Susan's intention to divorce Fenn. Susan raves on for the loss of her aborted twins, and Fenn suffers the agony, too. The sudden show-up of Chessie, the Chesapeake legendary sea-monster, serves as a divine revelation for Fenn and Susan to unknot their literary deadlock, to overcome their life crisis and finally to reverse their predicament. Sighting and pursuing Chessie redeem Susan and Fenn from their spiritual turbulence and strengthen them with the belief that they get divine inspiration from the rare sighting of the sea-monster, a contemporary avatar of leviathan. In terms of plot, their narrative "*A LEGENDARY SEA-MONSTER SWIMS THROUGH OUR STORY*" poses as a turning point in their strained story-telling. The epiphany comes first with Susan's naming of the sea-monster as Chessie and then with Susan and Fenn's ultimate solution to their creative stagnation right after their joint narrative on the sea-monster:

"'That sea-monster was important. There's a power I didn't know about, and now I think I've got it. Maybe I had it all along; that doesn't matter. You gave it to me by naming it. In fact, it's not mine: it's ours[...],' says Fenn in ecstasy to Susan"(351). *'It's our power and our voice, and what it's for is our story. Hoo! Everything's is coming so clear;' Fenn cries further with joy, 'we're plotting our own course now'"* (351-52).

Enlightened and becoming confident, Fenn realizes that their literary effort gets stuck in a bottleneck because

---

whereas the latter survives the surgery, overcomes the subsequent emotional turmoil and successfully conceives and gives birth to a brainchild.

"we didn't make the decisions we'd hoped to make on this sabbatical sail because the questions we were trying to decide were the wrong ones. No, excuse him: they're the right questions, but we had the wrong handle on them"(358).

After Fenn and Susan have sighted Chessie and got inspired, Fenn assures his wife that what his life with her has been for and about is writing a story. Fenn says:

*"Yet it's our story; it will be our story. What's more[...]**this story, our story, it's our house and our child**[...]We'll have made it, says determined Fenn, and we'll live in it. We'll even live by it. **It doesn't have to be about us—children aren't about their parents.** But our love will be in it, and our friendship too. This boat ride will be in it, somehow. It'll be about things coming around to where they started and then going on a little farther in a different way [...]"*(356-57, emphasis added).

The author/book relationship is traditionally compared to the father/son relationship. However, Fenn transforms this association into a *parents/children* relationship. This metaphoric transmutation denotes and underlines the concept of androgyny in that childbirth literally requires a union of male and female and giving birth to a brainchild in Susan and Fenn's case calls for their joint creative effort. Fenn's metaphor that he is like a sperm and Susan an egg meeting each other fully expresses their individuality and collaboration, their diversion and confluence and ultimately their androgynous unification— an ideal best betokened by the logo "Y" prevalent in *Sabbatical*. The androgynous harmony in formal pattern and rhyme scheme in *ca dao*, the oral folk lyrics of the Vietnamese (i.e. the *luc-bat* rhyming couplet demands the "male" couplets meet the "female" ones) sung by Eastwood Ho, also helps envision the notion of sexual equity in *Sabbatical*.

Fenn's two marriages— one fails and the other succeeds— also explain the importance of a harmonious marriage of maleness and femaleness to creative childbirth. Sleeping with Susan on their boat along the seashore of Key Island on a stormy night, Fenn makes into a story his tour with his ex-wife Marilyn Marsh and son Orrin in Spain. Fenn initiates the trip there in an attempt to produce a novel; nevertheless, the vacation ends up awfully. Fenn and Marilyn quarrel fiercely in public as they tour the Tajo de Ronda. Fenn recognizes that his marriage with Marilyn has come to the end and believes that he cannot make a writer. In despair, Fenn throws his manuscript down into the gorge. Fenn tells Susan that his story of the boina is *"the story of the story that taught me I couldn't write stories"* (44). That is to say, a failed marriage metaphorically signals an abortive creative endeavor. In contrast, Fenn and Susan's successful marriage — especially with their ultimate resolution to their crisis, both marital and literary (narrative) — strengthens their collaborative creative effort, helps the couple narrators break through the bottleneck in their narrative, and "finishes" their story of their *Sabbatical*. Fenn's remark in ecstasy that he and Susan are "literary twins" illustrates the power of androgyny in bringing about their literary triumph:

"We literal twins, he [Fenn] declares, might justly turn the tables and use schizophrenia as the image of our plural selves, narcissism as the image of our love for another; for we know to the bone the truth of Aristophanes's wonderful fancy: that we are each of us the fallen moiety of a once-seamless whole. But so far from being doomed to seek forever and in vain our missing half, whether of the same or of opposite sex, we know that half supremely well, perhaps better than anyone normally knows anyone else; and our habit of wholeness ought to make us ideal partners, especially for another twin, compatible as left hand and right—even if, perhaps particularly if, our original half falls by the way"(332).

When Susan and Fenn are painstakingly struggling for the final note to their sabbatical (their life) and *Sabbatical* (their story), Susan's timely suggestion that

"[i]f that's going to be our story, then let's begin it at the end and end at the beginning, so we can go on forever"

enlightens the pensive Fenn and, accordingly, leads them to "complete" their story by giving a loophole to their circular narrative

(365).[15] At this point, Max F. Schulz's interpretation of Susan simply as a Muse mediating Fenn's creativity invites questioning and requires clarification:

"In fact Fenn relies heavily upon Susan's literary expertise to pilot his amateurish way through the intricacies of plotting. She figures for Fenn in his story as the yarning Scheherazade does for the Genie Barth in 'Dunyazadiad,' and Lady Amherst for Ambrose in Letters— his muse, mentor, mistress, and (in Fenn's case) wife, 'Vera to his Vladimir'[...] they tend to think of their literary labors as a collaborative effort and to use plural pronominal self-references"(Schulz 1990:137).

By Schulz's definition, Susan is a collaborator because she acts as the Muse, the inspiring object, to Fenn. Nevertheless, Susan is not merely a catalyst or a vehicle for Fenn's imagination and creativity; she is a co-author. The following quote of the dual narrators' concluding dialogue shall illustrate Schulz's misreading of the context as well as his misquoting of the text:

"[...]if she's [Susan herself] to play muse to his bard, Vera to his Vladimir No no no, her husband protests. It's not my story about us; it's our story about the whole thing, Big Bang to Black hole"(360).

Susan does not simply play the inspiring Muse, nor does she function just as a medium for male creativity. Susan is an independent subject who co-writes with Fenn their *Sabbatical.* Thus argued, the androgynous narrative paradigm comes to the fore and becomes most manifested in Barth's conclusion to the novel *Sabbatical*. Fenn's earlier remark that *"I'm not **all** male, nor you all female. Just mainly"* finds its fulfillment in the end (169).

And this realization echoes and embodies Woolf's ideal in *A Room of One's Own* that a great literary mind is an androgynous mind, a fusion of "*the two sexes in the mind*"— that is, it is man-womanly and woman-manly (96). In *Sabbatical*, Barth illustrates this androgynous mind with the

---

[15] In his "Foreword" to *Lost in the Funhouse*, Barth adopts the term "Möbius strip" to elucidate this type of narrative structure— "*a circuit with a twist to it.*" John Barth, "Foreword," *Lost in the Funhouse*, (N.Y.: Anchor, 1988): vii.

hero and heroine's co-creativity. Given the metamorphosis from an androcentric narrative paragidm to an androgynous one, we can infer that there is genuine "pen," great creativity, rather than "penis," patriarchal inscription, in Barth's fiction. And this androgynous discourse marks a watershed in the evolution of Barth's fiction.

WORKS CITED

Barth, John. *The Floating Opera and The End of the Road.* N.Y.: Doubleday, 1988.

---. "Foreword." *Lost in the Funhouse*. N.Y.: Anchor, 1988. v-viii.

---. "Dunyazadiad." *Chimera*. N.Y.: Fawcett Crest, 1972.

---. *Sabbatical: A Romance*. Normal: Dalkey Archive Press, 1996.

de Beauvoir, Simone. *The Second Sex*. N. Y.: Vintage, 1989.

Bedetti, Gabriella. "Women's Sense of the Ludicrous in John Barth's 'Dunyazadiad'." *Studies in American Humor* 4.1-2 (1985): 74-81.

Bowen, Zack. *A Reader's Guide to John Barth*. Connecticut & London: Greenwood, 1994.

Davis, Cynthia. "Heroes, Earth Mothers and Muses: Gender Identity in Barth's Fiction." *The Centennial Review* 24 (1980): 309-21.

Fogel, Stan & Gordon Slethaug. *Understanding John Barth*. Columbia: U of South Carolina P, 1990.

Friedman, Susan Stanford. "Creativity and the Childbirth Metaphor: Gender Difference in Literary Discourse." *Speaking of Gender*. Intro. & Ed. Elaine Showalter. N.Y.: Routledge, 1989. 73-100.

Harris, Charles B. *Passionate Virtuosity: The Fiction of John Barth*. Urbana & Chicago: U of Illinois P, 1983.

Noland, Richard W. "John Barth and the Novel of Comic Nihilism." *Critical Essays on John Barth*. Ed. Joseph J. Waldmeir. Boston: G. K. Hall, 1980. 14-29.

Owen, Craig. "The Discourse of Others: Feminists and Postmodernism." *The Anti-Aesthetic: Essays on Postmodern Culture*. Ed. & Intro. Hal Foster. N.Y.: The New Press, 1998. 57-82.

Reilly, Charlie. "An Interview with John Barth." *Contemporary Literature* 22.1 (1981):1-23.

Schulz, Max F. *The Muses of John Barth*. Baltimore: Johns Hopkins UP, 1990.

Showalter, Elaine. "Introduction: The Rise of Gender." *Speaking of Gender*. Ed.Elaine Showalter. N.Y.: Routledge, 1989. 1-13.

Slethaug, Gordon E. "Floating Signifiers in John Barth's *Sabbatical.*" *Modern Fiction Studies* 33.4 (1987): 647-55.

Tharpe, Jac. *John Barth: The Comic Sublimity of Paradox*. Pref. Harry T. Moore.Carbondale and Edwardsville: Southern Illinois UP, 1974.

Tobin, Patricia. *John Barth and the Anxiety of Continuance*. Philadelphia: U of Pennsylvania P, 1992.

Woolf, Virginia. *A Room of One's Own*. London: Penguin, 1945.

II.3 Michal Peprník: The Late (Postmodern) Mohican: From the Spectacle of Revenge to a Show

Film has a parasitic relationship to literature. The film adaptation can never capture the complexity of literary characterization and of plot development, and its visual representation seldom corresponds to our own imagination. It can never include all the material contained in the literary work, it has to be explicit where novel can be implicit and suggestive. Film adaptations of J. F. Cooper's novel *The Last of the Mohicans* (1826) provide a good example. Since I am a reader by profession, I will approach the film adaptation mostly from the reader's perspective. I am aware of the reductive character of my approach because the film is primarily a visual medium. On the other hand, the film depends on text, on a story, and it depends on it so vitally that it frequently turns to classic novels for better or worse.

Even though we may argue with Jacques Derrida that any kind of inscription of meaning upon the body of the text comprises a large amount of violence (*Of Grammatology*), yet the amount of violence committed against Cooper's novel *The Last of the Mohicans* is truly staggering. Reading the plot summaries of old adaptations, one may suspect a conspiracy. Not only that the film scripts do not do justice to Cooper, they seem to take revenge on him for some unspeakable offences he unwittingly committed. No classic work of American literature has inspired so many film adaptations (24 films).[1] Hardly any classic has been subjected to such drastic rewritings as if *The Last of the Mohicans* was a training battle site where every imaginable combination, every thinkable deviation has been tried. Beginning with a 15-minute one-reel silent movie from 1911, where Cora did not die, to film adaptations in which Uncas survives or is absent as a character, or in which Chingachgook, his father, is missing, both ladies survive, or one is absent.

---

[1] See Edward Harris, "Cooper on Film," *James Fenimore Cooper Society Webpage.* 18 Jan. 2002 http://www.oneonta.edu/~cooper/drama/film.html.

As if there was something in the novel that is both appealing and unsatisfactory, demanding *"an interpretative completion"*(Baker, Sabin 1996: 33)[2], a change, a rewriting. As if the violence of the book bred more violence and called for another cycle of revenge. Therefore I want to compare the novelistic and film treatments of the motif of revenge in order to understand the cultural logic or rationale behind it. I do not know whether I will manage to escape the warpath of the signifier of revenge, whether I can avoid the reduplication of previous strategies and stratagems of revenge[3], but at least I fancy, *my cause is noble. Justice for Cooper*!

Michael Mann's *The Last of the Mohicans* (1992) is the example of the latest and most radical mutilation of the original text. The motif of revenge is expanded ad absurdum. Surprisingly, no matter how postmodern Mann's script may look, it is a remake of an old remake. It is largely based on the 1936 film version (director George B. Seitz), itself a remake of Seitz's 1924 silent movie). The 1936 script is responsible for the most radical shifts in the plot and characterization, and consequently also for the simplification of the political agenda. Among the main changes one will find that Hawk-eye, in the novel a fatherly figure at the age of forty, is changed into a young man (Daniel Day-Lewis) in the film—obviously to make him fit for a Hollywood romance. Unlike Cooper's Hawk-eye, who considers himself a man of no cross (that is, a white man), Hawk-eye from the film regards himself an Indian, and he addresses the elderly and rather stout Chingachgook, "Father". The English are depicted as unscrupulous villains, and the settlers, who practically figure only by name in the novel, become unwitting victims of the power-games of the two Colonial superpowers, the French and the English. The film has Duncan Heyward, an officer of the English army, propose to Cora but he is turned down, burned at stake, while she falls in

---

[2] Martin Baker and Roger Sabin, *The Lasting of the Mohicans: History of an American Myth* (Jackson: UP of Mississippi, 1996). Henceforth as *The Lasting.*

love with Hawk-eye. In the novel she is an object of interest of Magua, the bad Indian, and of Uncas, the good Indian. The film, however, offers an affair between Uncas and blond Alice. Both die in the film, while in the novel the blond Alice marries good Duncan.

Tradition of Revenge

Revenge is an ancient cultural notion and ancient literary motif. There is no way of doing justice to the notion of revenge. Both *Encyclopaedia Britanica* and *Americana* choose to shun this issue, and, as usual, it is practically impossible to find a clear, concise definition. Revenge should be probably studied against the background of similiar concepts such as retaliation, retribution and vengeance. Historically, the pattern of revenge is connected to an older system,

"characteristic of multicentric societies in which numerous relatively small social units practice 'self-government,' protecting their members from injury by outsiders."[4]

Revenge, in general, denotes *"retaliation for injuries or wrongs, insult,"* and I would add, it entails a personal response. The injured, or afflicted individual or his defenders act outside the institutional frame of repressive and retributive justice of the state. The personal retaliation can take numerous forms— it can demand an exact return (an eye for an eye), it can be *excessive* (an eye for two eyes, ears and the nose, or, cut it all— the whole head). Cooper's Hawk-eye promises Duncan Heyward that if the Hurons get his scalp, he will kill one Huron for each hair of Heyward's scalp (22: 249)— unless Duncan had been bald or thin-haired like Roderick Usher, it would have kept Hawk-eye busy for several lifetimes (a human scalp has about 80,000 hairs).

The retributive pattern of revenge served as a deterrent in many decentralized societies. In his *Oregon Trail,* Francis Parkman mentions

---

[3] See Barbara Johnson, *The Critical Difference* (1980; Baltimore: The Johns Hopkins UP, 1982).

[4] Ronald Broude, "Revenge and Revenge Tragedy in Renaissance England," *Renaissance Quarterly,* 28,1 (Spring, 1975): 38-58.

the example of a young distinguished Sioux war-chief, who kidnapped a few dozens of Indian women, but no one dared to punish him because apart from being a formidable warrior he had twenty younger brothers, all ready to revenge his eventual death. On the other hand, there were limits to the effect of determent— in spite of all those 20 potential avengers, their father was killed by his enemies because he grew too powerful and authoritative.[5] Even though it is generally believed that personal revenge is decidedly an evidence of a primitive stage of reflection, it is unfortunately still part of our life.

Revenge in Literature

Revenge is one of the most favourite motifs in literature. Revenge plots flourished in Ancient Greek and Roman drama; Seneca's tragedies of revenge were made popular in England by Thomas Kyd, who in turn influenced Shakespeare as evidenced in *Hamlet.* Although T. S. Eliot argued that *Hamlet* is a bad revenge play full of flaws and tended to regard Hamlet as a raving maniac unable to take a quick and decisive action, Hamlet can be seen as a very cruel avenger— he does not hesitate, he only waits for the right moment when he could strike Claudius in the act of committing a sin and thus send him straight to hell's fires. Let us recall that Hamlet's father was killed without the possibility to receive last relief and make a confession.

Powerful revenge plots dominate in *The Merchant of Venice,* or in *Othello.* The popularity of tragedy of revenge achieved its heights in Jacobean drama, in the so-called tragedies of blood.[6]

American literature became especially responsive to tales of revenge— the revenge was a hard reality on the frontier and it led to many excesses in the conflicts between the Indians and white

[5] The famous Iroquois League came to being as the means of stopping the endless feuds, which were decimating the Iroquois. The founders of the League introduced a system of compensations and payments for injuries and offences.

[6] The concept of tragedy of revenge is, according to Ronald Broude, an early 20th century invention, Renaissance did not know the tragedy of revenge, only so called tragedy of blood.

settlers.Revenge provided steam for some of the greatest American classics, *The Scarlet Letter, Huckleberry Finn, The House of Seven Gables, Moby-Dick*, *Billy Budd.* Cooper exploits the motif of revenge in *Satanstoe, Wyandotté, The Deerslayer, The Oak Openings.* Cooper's rather positive attitude to Indians inspired a whole school of tales of dark revenge, for example *Nick of the Woods* by Robert Montgomery Bird, or *Logan* by John Neal.

In his *Beneath the American Renaissance,* David S. Reynolds shows that tales of dark and gruesome revenge enjoyed wide circulation in American sensational press and popular literature, either as semi-authentic narratives of criminals or as entirely fictive accounts as early as the 1830s. The tales of revenge usually follow the traditional narrative pattern as described by Ronald Broude:

"Revenge tragedy is usually understood to center around a figure who conceives himself to have been seriously wronged, and who, overcoming obstacles both within and outside himself, contrives eventually to exact retribution, becoming in the process as depraved as those by whom he has been wronged"(Broude 1975:38).

This definition, however, does not exactly apply to Cooper. He is always interested in the kind of revenge that might be classified as *excessive.* The revenge is attributed to the Indians. Those who inflict the injury follow a different concept of law and punishment, and do not act out of malice— in all three major cases the offence is the same: an Indian was flogged, in two cases deservedly according to the white law in *Wyandotté*, a punishment for getting drunk while on duty in *Satanstoe* (the first volume of *Littlepage Trilogy*), a black servant captures and flogs a Wyandotte chief, and thus brings the Indian revenge on his master and his associates. Interestingly, the film does not accept Cooper's conception of excessive revenge and returns to the more ancient classic formula of tragedy of revenge— the offence is made as hideous as the revenge.

Revenge in Cooper's Novel

Cooper's novel bears resemblance to the tragedy of revenge. In fact, it makes explicit intertextual connections with the tragedy of revenge through allusions to John Milton's *Prince of Darkness*, brooding on the ways of taking revenge (*Paradise Lost),* or more significantly, in the epigraph from William Shakespeare's *The Merchant of Venice,* wherein Shakespeare relates Magua to Shylock.

A structural analysis of the plot reveals that the motif of revenge is of key importance both in the novel and the film. The chief devious avenger, Magua, is the chief engine of the plot: he keeps kidnapping the ladies; he engineers the massacre at Fort Henry, and frustrates the European attempts to introduce more civilized manners of resolving the conflict. And last, but not the least, he kills Uncas, the last of the Mohicans, and extinguishes the last spark of hope for the Indians.[7]

Magua's Motivation for Revenge

Magua is driven by revenge for the wrongs he suffered and by high ambition to regain his lost position in his native tribe— he was expelled from his native tribe (the Hurons) because of drinking and he joined the Mohawks, an enemy tribe and an ally of the English army. On top of that, colonel Munro had him flogged in public (again because of drinking). Although his punishments were not undeserved, Magua blames the whites. Cooper used these two punishments to display cultural differences. Both punishments are legitimate inside the legal systems but invalid outside those systems. When Cora, a dark lady whom Magua wants for a wife, objects that the flogging was a just punishment, Magua vehemently does not agree. While flogging was a standard punishment for serious offences in the English army, for an Indian it is highly

---

[7] Uncas's sudden appearance among the Delawares is viewed as an event which is part of the mythic cycle of ages, an advent of a new age, of a tomorrow that never was. According to the old Tamenund prophecy Uncas's arrival was to change the tide of history and stop the gradual decline of the Indians and was to restore them to their original greatness and fame. Magua makes sure that the hope dies very soon.

excessive because it is considered as the most humiliating punishment, even worse than death by torture. Magua also refuses to take responsibility for his acting while being under the influence of alcohol. He blames the whites because they brought a vice (fire water) that the Indians had not known before and could not resist (How strangely familiar is this complaint!):

"Is it justice to make evil, and then punish for it! Magua was not himself; it was the fire-water that spoke and acted for him, but Munro did not believe it" (9: 116).

On the other hand, his argumentation is weakened by the Indians who were in contact with the whites and did not drink (for instance the two last Mohicans). Even though Cooper provides some justification for Magua's revenge, the concept of his revenge testifies to Magua's twisted character. His revenge is mean. Instead of hitting Colonel Munro directly, he uses terrorists' favourite strategy— kidnapping the innocent. He kidnaps colonel Munro's daughters because he knows very well that this is the most vulnerable spot in Munro. He wants to keep Cora as a wife for several purposes, for example as a safeguard of his well-being, as a substitute and compensation for the losses he suffered, but, primarily, for the malicious feeling that he can keep the edge of his knife on Munro's soul, as he puts it. And last, but not least, since Magua lived in both cultures, he knows that for a white lady of genteel background the fate of an Indian wife is the fate of humiliation, enslavement and debasement. He knows that and relishes this notion that Cora will work in the field and make his beans for dinner, for example, not to speak of the unspeakable.

Film Adaptation of *The Last of the Mohicans*

Mann's adaptation[8] lends much more space to the revenge— not only it widens the justification and supplies more convincing reasons for Magua's revenge, but it also increases the number of objects of revenge. In other words, Magua's status of justified avenger is considerably

[8] The script of the film is available on the internet: *The Last of the Mohicans.* 18 Jan. 2002. http://www.moviescripts.de/html/script/lastmohican.html.

strengthened. As if flogging was found too weak a motivation, the scriptwriters added a few more truly beastly afflictions. Magua reveals to the French general Montcalm that his native village was burned and his children were killed by a unit of English army led by colonel Munro in person (a motif absent in the book). Since the family is universally sacred, any attack against one's own family justifies a retaliation in popular imagination (See the recent film *The Patriot*). This kind of personal and intimate grievance lends an edge to the revenge. Magua's loss of family represents such a powerful cultural reason, widely abused in Hollywood revenge plots, that it practically transforms him into an object of our sympathy, while it reduces the English colonial army officers into shameless barbarians (another obvious advantage of such a reduction of Heyward and Munro is to prepare the viewer for their bloody disposal during Magua's revenge).

The script extends Magua's **scope of revenge** as well— in the film he gets not only more justification, but also more revenge. His whole plan for revenge is less sophisticated, less psychological, less subtle, less in the spirit of Le Lenard Subtil (Magua's nickname), but more blunt, more brutal, more primitive, more explicit, and more spectacular.He does not plan to keep Cora as a hostage, wife and the tool of torturing her father, colonel Munro. He wants to kill them all, he wants "destroy his seed". His original plan is to kill the ladies first so that Munro suffers more:

"Before he dies Magua will put his children under the knife so that the Grey Hair will see his seed wiped out forever".

Nevertheless, Magua is pragmatic about his revenge— when he has a chance to kill Munro, he does it. When he brings his captives to the Huron camp, he wants to burn the ladies in fire "*so all can share in this*", and sell Duncan Heyward to the French for a ransom. Cooper's Magua was willing to send fair and childish Alice back to her father in order to keep him alive for the mental torments— a loss of both daughters would send him to the grave too soon. Magua is given a lot of satisfaction in the film— unlike Shakespeare's Shylock, he gets his pound of flesh. He is also a man straight enough to kill Colonel Munro and a savage brutish enough to do it in the most appalling way— as he shoots Munro's horse, Munro becomes entrapped under the horse and Magua cuts his heart out alive and wields the bloody heart as a trophy.[9] However, not only colonel Munro, but also Duncan Heyward and Alice die in consequence of Magua's revenge, even though not by his own hand. The film also treats a dubious privilege of the revenge on Magua differently as well, or, in other words, his punishment. In the film this privilege is delegated to Chingachgook (a pattern first employed in the 1936 version and also found in the 1977 version, referred to in literature as a "*boy-scout adaptation*"). Obviously, this shift is part of the general policy to give more space and significance to the Indians but it has also somewhat less desirable implications— it keeps the white hands clean and white. But there is another powerful reason for this choice— aesthetics of violence, the **visual spectacle.**

The Revenge as a Spectacle

The postmodern society is frequently characterized as a society of spectacle.[10] This concept is usually associated with Jean Baudrillard but it has been widely adopted in postmodern theory. Fredrick Jameson is one those who speak of the collapse of the relationship between the signifier and the signified as a consequence of the schizophrenic disintegration of the continuous personal identity, a loss of sense of historicity. We are left with the shining, oppressive or obsessive, hallucinatory signifiers, material signs that radiate their presence but lack meaning. The referent, the real

[9] The morbid obsession of American writers and scriptwriters with guts and intestines ripped open has in fact a longer history than one might suppose, as David S. Reynolds has proved in his excellent study of the 19th century sensational literature, *Beneath the American Renaissance* (1988). I take it as a trope for the obsessive Puritan investigative soul-searching: what is inside has to be outside because we need to be informed about what we cannot see. You must "have guts" in American— if you don't, you are obviously no man any more.

[10] In 1967 Guy Debord wrote a book *The Society of Spectacle* where he outlined this concept. He was a member of a French group of Situationist theorists. See also Zygmunt Bauman, *Tekutá moderna* (Praha: Mladá fronta, 2002).

object, had been long lost in the process of signifying practice, as our experience becomes increasingly mediated:

"Note that as temporal continuities break down, the experience of the present becomes powerfully, overwhelmingly vivid and 'material': the world comes before the schizophrenic with heightened intensity, bearing a mysterious and oppressive charge of effect, glowing with hallucinatory energy"(Jameson 1983:120).

Since the signifier loses its signified, it changes into an image, and the referents cease to be real objects and become other images (123).

However, in his *Ecstasy of Communication* (1983)[11] Jean Baudrillard argues that we no longer live in a society of spectacle. The society of spectacle was the consumer society that *"lived under the sign of alienation*". But now we live in a new stage, in networks, we are not alienated because we are connected— *"we live in the ecstasy of communication*" of which the mobile (cell) phone, internet and TV are now the most obvious examples.

The transformation of the society is demonstrated by examples of the collapse of older binary oppositions and the emergence of new ones. Probably the most important change is the loss of the public and private space, and the disappearance of the "scene and mirror". Baudrillard links it to the breakdown of the traditional subject/object relationship. The existence of the gap between the self and the other was a source of anxiety and alienation on one hand, but it also provided a sense of certainty that the Other exists, and thus also a sense of identity because we could use the other as a mirror. Now everything converges on the screen, the space of the real is practically gone, argues Baudrillard (probably more true for an academic than for an average man or woman who still spend considerable time in "live" social interaction):

"But today the scene and mirror no longer exist; instead, there is a screen and network. In place of the reflective transcendence of mirror and scene, there is nonreflecting surface, an immanent surface where

---

[11] Jean Baudrillard, "The Ecstasy of Communication", *The Anti-Aesthetic* 126-134.

operations unfold— the smooth operational surface of communication" (Baudrillard 1983:127).

One of the consequences of the disappearance of public space (the street, monument, market, scene) and private space are the loss of spectacle and the loss of secret, respectively. The opposition between them is

"*effaced in a sort of obscenity where the most intimate processes of our life become the virtual feeding ground of the media*"(130) .

Everything is available on the screen. Baudrillard calls it "*pornography of information and communication*"(130). Even though he uses the concept "*ecstasy of communication*", the ecstasy is "cold".

"*One thing is sure: the scene excites us, the obscene fascinates us. With fascination and ecstasy, passion disappears. Investment, desire, passion, seduction or again, according to Caillois, expression and competition— the hot universe. Ecstasy, obscenity, fascination, communication[...]the cold universe*"(132).

Cold Fascination and Hot Revenge

Let us accept for a while Baudrillard's revision of terminology and exchange a scene for an "*obscene*". There is however a problem with a substitution for a spectacle as a phenomenon of public space, embedded in a historical scene. If we decide to accept Baudrillard's assertion that there is no spectacle any more, we find ourselves truly in a void. What is it that we actually see? Just the screen? Positively, if it is switched off, but even then we can even see a reflection of ourselves like in "*the good old times of the consumer society*". If the screen is on, do we see merely "*images*"— as Jameson suggests?

I suggest we call the substitute for a spectacle a "show". What form then does the revenge take on the screen? The film as a visual medium naturally always craves for "spectacles" and "shows", and in that respect Mann's film adaptation can well satisfy our hunger.[12] The siege of the fort

[12] One can recall similar, stunned admiration for the spectacle of war in Tim O'Brien's short stories from the Vietnam War, *The Things They Carried*.

Henry is both a lavish show and a wonderful spectacle. While it looks like a celebration with fireworks, at the same time it tries to convey a sense of historic authenticity, offering more of the actual historical background than Cooper did (the film introduces American settlers who want to give up, shows also the Indians fighting alongside with the English, etc).

The act of revenge, however, is usually a private affair, a hot passionate event. If the acts of revenge are to operate as a spectacle or a show they need proper space and time. In Cooper the acts of revenge are too brief— the postmodern voyeur wants to relish this ultimate consummation of violence. In the novel Magua is shot by Hawk-eye— the act of punishment and retribution is brief, efficient and sufficient, and yet spectacular, exactly in the American style— airborne, struck by the extended arm of divine justice straight from the clear sky. A steady aim, swift bullet, and then we watch the effect: Magua shakes his fist in defiance and laughs in a demonic fashion, then loses his grip, and mortally wounded falls into the pit. The scene is "hot"— endowed with great emotional intensity that is embodied in the character of Hawk-eye. This man of steel is shaking all over, overwrought with emotions, unable to keep a steady aim until the right moment arrives, and he changes into the impersonal agent of justice. The moment of revenge is a poor satisfaction for the death of Uncas because his death is an event of mythic momentum, while his arrival among the Delaware opened a new dimension on history, his death closed it.

The film, however, needs more physical action and a longer spectacle of violence, a real show. However, no matter how long the film presentation is, it seems "cold". The critics noticed a somewhat un-American style of film shooting. One critic muses about the long close-ups presenting frequent expression of wonder or curiosity and fascination.[13] It

---

[13] *"It is as though all his characters have trouble expressing themselves. They are very inward and self-contained most of the time, not showing their feelings and desires through words or actions. Instead the camera in many scenes dwells long on the faces as people reveal by their very physicality what they are feeling... There seems to be a continual shifting between bewilderment and determination in the faces of characters"* (Barker and Sabin, *The Lasting* 109).

is true— the heroes are cool, they do not cry, they seem to be in control even when they are stirred by sexual passion or caught up in a fight or distress. Magua offers his hand to the white blond lady he has chosen for his squaw as she leans back to the edge of the pit until she slowly topples there. While in the novel the murder of Cora by a Huron warrior enraged Magua so much that he killed the murderer on the spot, in the film his companions are absent in this final scene, and his expression just conveys the sense of wonder, fascination and slight disbelief as well as in the act of his own death by the hand of Chingachgook. It is Magua's gaze that can be classified *obscene* in Baudrillard's sense. And his gaze is our gaze, puzzled, fascinated with the image that carries no historical or mythic weight. Uncas as well as Alice are marginal characters in the film, sympathetic but unimpressive. Chingachgook's revenge, the duel with Magua, absent in the novel, in all its gruesome physicality takes on an aesthetic dimension. In a dancelike combat Chingachgook delivers his deadly blow as if he were chopping a tree, we can hear the unpleasant thumping sound as his war-club fractures Magua's body. We watch the amazed disbelief in Magua's dark face as he drops to the rock floor. No shaking of fists, no demonic laughter.

The Underside of the Show of Revenge

When we reconsider the important shifts in the scenes of revenge in the film, we can discern another pattern.[14] Not only the revenge is more brutal and explicit. The distribution of revenge is conceived differently. Simply put, the revenge in the novel is given to Magua and Hawk-eye. In the film it goes to the Indians. They get more revenge. Both Magua and Chingachgook are allowed to have their moments of "sweet" bloody revenge— in the film, Magua kills Munro and cuts out his reeking heart (he takes his "*pound of flesh*"), he has the satisfaction of seeing Duncan Heyward burning at stake, and overcomes Uncas in a fair fight, giving him no chance. In turn, Chingachgook can take his fatherly revenge and kill

[14] The novel was conceived as a tragedy of revenge, with intertextual allusions to Shakespeare's *The Merchant of Venice* and John Milton's *The Paradise Lost*.

Magua in another fair fight. On one hand, we can view it as an attempt to put the Indians more into the center of action, but, in fact, since the main character is a white man and plays a more dominant role in the structure than in the novel, it appears more like a compensation for the suppression of the significance of the Mohicans in the film. But this desire for compensation has its dark side, and I wonder whether the filmmakers were aware of it. The scenes of violent revenge do not provide an aesthetic spectacle only, but they also operate as **rituals**, or, more specifically, as ritualistic enactments. Ritualistic enactments, in the Indian theory of dreams, were a technique of dealing with nightmares of capture and torture, or even dreams of desire. The enactments were carried out with utmost realism to prevent the nightmare from happening because the Indians believed, like many other nations, that some dreams are prophetic or express desires. La Farge reports that when an Iroquois warrior had a dream about being bound to a stake and tortured by the enemy, the Indians bound a dog to a stake, addressed the dog by the warrior's name and tortured and killed the dog as a replacement believing that the same event cannot happen twice in the near future.

The ritualistic enactment seems to be offered as a foil for the ethnic minorities— as if the film makers wanted to give the oppressed and the marginalized their chance of revenge, allow them to have their gory moment of triumph over the wicked Imperial whites and their collaborators who yield the power and rule over the settler (understand, a common man) and Indian alike. Ritual involves a sacrifice and invites to participation. The bloody pound of flesh, the fire, and the semi-ritualistic dance at the edge of the pit arrange the cultural forces in fiercely antagonistic dualities according to the master codes of dominance and exploitation. This is a politically simplistic perspective with bad guys the Colonialists and good guys the Americans, and Indians as the fringe (alternative) culture, caught between. This simplistic politicization is fundamentally foreign to Cooper. The ritual quality of the scenes of revenge offers a chance of releasing the rage not only to the ethnic minorities but also to those who can identify with them and view themselves also as subjects of victimization. It makes us accomplices in the culture wars between the victimized and the victimizers. The revenge ceases to be Magua's revenge and becomes also our revenge. We participate in the revenge plot against those scheming, unreliable, outlying imperialists, we tear their heart out and burn them in fire, and we suffer the poor blond fall into the pit because this is where the blonds now belong as long-standing symbols of sexual imperialism.

While in Cooper the revenge of the semi-Gothic villain was directed against the innocent, after the culture wars there are no innocents left. Even the blond girl is guilty now, guilty of being associated with a cultural idol, with sexual imperialism. The film makes the demons in order to exorcise them. The show of justified revenge is however double-edged. The film strongly legitimizes violence of revenge as a pattern of justice-making behavior and it suppresses the option of forgiveness and reconciliation, a perspective associated with female characters in Cooper and with the Quaker David Gamut in the novel. It is David Gamut that sternly reprimands Hawk-eye when he speaks of revenge if the Hurons kill David. And, very significantly, this character that stood for the Christian forgiveness in the book is missing in the film. Cora is also deprived of that function in the film. In Cooper's novel *The Wyandotté,* a heroine says to her lover, who wants to revenge his father,

"Defend us, as I know you will, but defend us like a Christian"(II, 12:164).

The level of ritualistic enactment shows that behind the hard layers of cool surfaces of popular culture, the old stereotypes still lurk and are employed in the very American way— *let it out*— erase the wall between the public and private space. Since the Puritan times, Americans have demanded a public confession— no secrets, no loitering, and instead of suppression a channeling, management and movement. In this sense it has always been a postmodern culture, where the spectacle can easily shift to a show.

WORKS CITED

Baker, M., Sabin, R. *The Lasting of the Mohicans: History of an American Myth* Jackson: UP of Mississippi, 1996.

Baudrillard, J. "The Ecstasy of Communication." *The Anti-Aesthetic. Essays on Postmodern Culture.* ed. Hal Foster. New York: The New Press, 1998. 126-134.

Broude, R. "Revenge and Revenge Tragedy in Renaissance England." *Renaissance Quarterly* 28:1(Spring 1975): 38-58.

Cooper, J.F. *The Last of the Mohicans.* 18 Jan. 2002. http://www.moviescripts.de/html/script/lastmohican.html

Cooper, J.F. *Wyandotté; or, the Hutted Knoll.* Philadelphia: Lea & Blanchard, 1843.

Harris, E. "Cooper on Film." *James Fenimore Cooper Society Webpage.* 18 Jan. 2002 http://www.oneonta.edu/~cooper/drama/film.html

Jameson, F. "Postmodernism and Consumer Society." *The Anti-Aesthetic. Essays on Postmodern Culture.* ed. Hal Foster. New York: The New Press, 1998. 111-125.

Johnson, B. *The Critical Difference.* Baltimore: The Johns Hopkins UP, 1982.

PART III

DRAMA AND MUSIC

III.I Zoe Detsi-Diamanti: Visions of *Blackness*: Ideology and the *Other* in George L. Aiken's *Uncle Tom's Cabin* (1853) and Dion Boucicault's *The Octoroon* (1859)

> Seeing what happens in the world, might one not say that the European is to men of other races what man is to the animals? He makes them serve his convenience, and when he cannot bend them to his will he destroys them. In one blow oppression has deprived the descendants of the Africans of almost all the privileges of humanity.
>
> (Alexis de Tocqueville, *Democracy in America* 317).

In the efforts to identify and stabilize both nation and identity, post-revolutionary American political ideology became rooted deeply in the republican principles of freedom and equality, thus giving Americans a sense of national unity and homogeneity and creating a facade of an orderly social hierarchy. Republican rhetoric, which rested on the assumptions of private virtue and public morality and the willingness of the people to subject themselves to the common good, carefully concealed the new nation's tendency to exclude the "less civilized" races, the Indians and the African-Americans, free and slave, from all public discussions of national identity. As Robert E. Shalhope has observed in his analysis of early American thought and culture, by the end of the eighteenth century

"*cries of republican equality became ever more insistent at the very time that Americans rigidly excluded blacks from their society, decimated Indian tribes in an attempt to transform them into republican citizens, restricted women to a separate, limited sphere, and created a markedly stratified society"* (137).[1]

Particularly in the case of southern slaves, ambivalent feelings regarding their presence in the American society betrayed the essential ambiguity and blatant inconsistency of white America's credo: the love of liberty, equality for all and progress. The enslavement of African-Americans threatened the viability of the republican experiment and exposed its hypocrisy and autocratic nature. That is why slavery could only be justified within the context of a hegemonic discourse that framed blacks into an image of racial inferiority, in constant need of guidance and paternalistic care. The question of slavery puzzled the Founding Fathers of the new nation who were determined to build a society that preserved and consolidated a kind of liberty and happiness that only those people deemed competent for self-rule could enjoy. For John Adams, slavery was a "black cloud" hanging over America and haunting him for his entire political life (*The Adams-Jefferson Letters*, Feb. 3, 1821), while Thomas Jefferson— though unusual for a slave-owning southerner— wrestled with the issue of slavery publicly from the time of the American Revolution. As a matter of fact, Jefferson voiced the general ambivalence towards blacks in that he assailed slavery, on the one hand, as the *"great political and moral evil"* of the land of liberty, while, on the other, praised the *"mild treatment"* accorded to slaves by their white masters. Jefferson believed that the problem of slavery would be extremely difficult to solve and interracial harmony impossible to achieve as

"deep rooted prejudices entertained by the whites; ten thousand recollections, by the blacks, of the injuries they have sustained .... [would] produce convulsions which will probably never end but in the extermination of one or the other race" (qtd. in Burstein 160).

---

[1] Adherence to republican principles allowed early Americans to view themselves as committed to the harmony, order and communal well-being of a republican society while actively creating an aggressive, individualistic one. For more information, see, Burstein and Matthews.

Like the majority of eighteenth-century Americans, Jefferson did not doubt that slavery as an institution was immoral, yet his commitment to human equality seems to have rested on the assumption that social equality was founded in nature. If nature itself had made certain groups inferior, then they were presumably excluded from the complete range of rights properly belonging to those who were born equal.[2]

As the nineteenth century progressed, the new nation's unconscious impulse to expand unleashed the forces of imperialism and cultural exclusion. On the one hand, the unrelenting drive across the American continent in the name of Manifest Destiny and, on the other, the ever-increasing need for immigrant and slave labor hands to fuel the burgeoning industrialism set off what Timothy Powell has called "the powerful forces of monoculturalism which sought to counter the increasing cultural diversity of the nation by legislatively constricting the boundaries of *"American citizenship"* (11). As a result, violent forces of racist exclusion meant that the Indians would be either *assimilated* or *removed* and the immigrants' rights severely circumscribed. As for the African-Americans, the issue of nationality and national identity became even more perplexing and complicated as America's conflicted will to empire entailed the preservation and extension of slavery. Gradually, the institution of slavery became the most divisive issue separating the country into "two competing cultural nationalisms" and bringing *"the nation closer to the brink of Civil War"* (Powell 13-4). Slavery and the unresolved dilemma of whether blacks should be freed or recolonized in Africa fragmented the antebellum American society.[3] As early as the 1850s, the

[2] Although he denied any passion or prejudice of his own, Jefferson felt an instinctive aversion towards blacks based on their skin color and considered them inferior in reasoning ability and intellect. He thought that freed slaves were extremely difficult to assimilate into white American society and that is why he championed the recolonization of blacks beyond America's limits.

[3] In the first decades of the nineteenth century, the American Colonization Society (ACS) advocated a policy of gradual emancipation of blacks, with the newly freed slaves returned to Africa, their native land. Such policies, however, betrayed, on the one hand, the general anxiety over the fact that freed blacks would naturally leave the South and migrate north into the *free* states where they were also unwelcome,

enactment of the Fugitive Slave Law, which compelled Harriet Beecher Stowe to write *Uncle Tom's Cabin* revealing the horrors of slavery to millions of readers, galvanized the already existing abolitionist sentiments, while, at the same time, made it clear that slavery implicated the whole of American nation.

The ceaseless interplay of the concepts of cultural exclusion and inclusion became an inextricable feature of American identity defining in a way the ideological parameters of the nation's interpretation of its own contradictions and ambivalences.[4] The new nation's innermost fears of multicultural disunity and racial intermixing exacerbated the already perplexing question of just who the *"We, the people"* actually included. With the growing strength of the abolition movement and the terrifying prospect that four million African-Americans might be set free, the impulse to cultural exclusion greatly contradicted the basic tenet of *the Declaration of Independence* that *"All men are created equal."*[5] Frederick Douglass, in the 1852 "The Meaning of July Fourth for the Negro" address, poignantly stressed the essential contradiction of American ideology and its Constitutional manifesto as he uttered:

"To drag a man in fetters into the grand illuminated temple of liberty and call upon him to join in joyous anthems is inhuman mockery and sacrilegious irony" (189).

The ideological conflict between the nation's cultural and racial diversity and its insistent will to homogeneity and consensus is more

---

and, on the other, American society's wishful thinking to remain a *white man's country*.

[4] In the first decades of the nineteenth century, the major political parties avoided the slavery issue and postponed any action on the slavery question at all. Men like Daniel Webster and Henry Clay, even though they disliked slavery, feared that its potential effect might prove disruptive for the Union. According to Eric Foner, both the Whigs and the Democrats accepted slavery in the South and supported the Compromise of 1850 in order to avoid dividing their constituencies (187-9).

[5] It must be noted that antislavery sentiment was not truly altruistic since many whites objected to the idea of assimilating millions of freed slaves into white American society. There were also those who in fact dreaded that in such case either race war or amalgamation would follow. See, Dillon and Richards.

implicitly, but just as pervasively, reflected in the American drama of the ante-bellum period.[6] The politics of race and its ideological ambiguities are captured by the theatre of the time, which, in the words of Jeffrey D. Mason, was *"an intricate and reflexive exercise in cultural self-definition"* (1993: 2). To the extent that the impact and centrality of the theatre as an indomitable cultural force cannot be underestimated, early American drama became a central medium of the nation's self-representation, an explicit site for performing national identity, for debating the issues, rhetoric, and the images that constituted national ideology and the concept of national character. The complex interplay between text and audience members amidst the codes and conventions of a given social context involves, on the one hand, the way audiences distill meaning from a performance in relation to their own cultural background, and, on the other, the social role of the theatre that legitimates, promotes, or even challenges a given ideology. In the case of American theatre, nineteenth-century drama made an effort at reproducing the constructed image of "America" as a nation of freedom-loving and righteous citizens, as the land of promise and opportunity. American theatre was in fact part of the overall republican experiment and contributed greatly to the creation and dissemination of an ideology that transcended the reality of America and operated on the plane of imagination.[7] This is precisely the aim of this paper: to explore how early American theatre consciously or unconsciously reflected the ambiguities of American society and rhetoric as it wavered between antithetical notions of reality/imagination, exclusion/inclusion, heterogeneity/homogeneity, repression/ opportunity. It is of particular interest to examine how nineteenth-century American

---

[6] this idea of the promotion of a single unifying ideology, see Bercovitch.

[7] Literary scholar Donald E. Pease, in his analysis of national narrative as a means of creating a nation by constructing imaginary relations to actual sociopolitical conditions, argues that "national narrative produced national identities by way of a social symbolic order that systematically separated an abstract, disembodied subject from resistant materialities, such as race, class, and gender" (3-4).

drama reinforced or undermined social structures, political functions and cultural symbols.[8]

In the analysis of early American plays, one cannot disregard the fact that the predominant dramatic form and theatrical style of the nineteenth-century was melodrama. Moving beyond the formal characteristics of melodrama as such and avoiding a formalist position that privileges only aesthetics, one should read American melodrama as a manifestation of the myths and ideological codes of American society and culture. The classic pattern of melodrama, its Manichean vision with its insistence on what Peter Brooks has termed *"the dramaturgy of virtue misprized and eventually recognized,"* seems to have fitted well into the overall republican schema of American society, into the democratic dream of the creation of a virtuous world with virtuous citizens (27).[9] Nineteenth-century melodrama, with its promise for the restoration of virtue and the moral, social, and domestic order, reassured the American audiences of the time that, though their fears of social disruption were valid, their optimism would eventually be justified. Popular melodramatic plays like George L. Aiken's *Uncle Tom's Cabin* (1853) and Dion Boucicault's *The Octoroon* (1859) greatly appealed to nineteenth-century American audiences not only because they successfully manipulated the techniques and conventions of melodrama, but because they endorsed the values

---

[8] For Jeffery D. Mason, the American stage becomes "a platform where players and audience may enact conceptions of identity and community, where 'America' becomes both the subject and the consequence of artistic, cultural, and social negotiation"(1999: 4).

[9] The melodramatic world, which is composed of binary oppositions, provides a paradoxical means of resolving fundamental contradictions, enacting a dark fantasy for its sentimental audiences that concerns society's dissolution and its ultimate salvation, thus affirming their values and their faith in social harmony and order. Melodrama operates in relation to ideology, myth and representation, articulating the values and codes of the dominant culture in which it is produced, offering allegorical action that conveys a world view, and, of course, inevitably reflecting the ambiguities and ambivalences of a certain social structure and ideology through its illusory finale that vanquishes evil and returns the virtuous to the condition they cherish and deserve. For more information regarding the conventions, aesthetics, and ideology of melodrama, see Brooks and Hays.

and ideological codes of the hegemonic culture.[10] By the 1850s, the emergence of the bourgeoisie signaled the beginning of a number of changes in American society and culture. The expansion of capitalism and the introduction of a new acquisitive and rationalistic individualism undercut the ideals of republican citizenship and legitimated a culture that catered for the interests of the new business class. In the theatre, the dominance of this new business class of industrialists and financiers was confirmed with the production of moral reform plays and sensation melodramas which encouraged family attendance and segregated the *respectable* from the lower classes of society.[11] In an era of increasing industrialization, bourgeois consumption was reflected in the various technological developments in the American theatre and the unquenchable thirst for more spectacle and scenic effects. As the theatre changed to fulfill the new social needs, the emerging bourgeoisie sought to strengthen its power and consolidate the new industrial morality of hard work, temperance and perseverance as essential prerequisites for achieving self-made success. Sentimental domesticity, family unity, piety and tolerance, were enthusiastically applauded by the nineteenth-century American audiences who indulged in an illusion of security and stability in an otherwise economically fluid social reality.

In the case of the theatrical representation of black characters, nineteenth-century American plays promoted a vision of 'blackness' that appeared equally problematic with the wider political ideology of inclusion/exclusion as it defined the African-American within the limits of a hegemonic discourse that constructed the African as Other. In the American society, blacks were rhetorically positioned within a framework of values dominated by the mainstream culture of whites who regarded the African as barbaric, heathen, and inferior, in constant need of guidance and instruction. As a matter of fact, the

[10] For the role and power of hegemonic culture and discourse, see Gramsci and Williams.

[11] For more information, see McConachie and Levine.

"representation of the African as Other signified prenotypical and cultural characteristics as evidence of this inferiority and the attributed condition of Africans therefore constituted a measure of European progress and civilization" (Miles 30).

Of course, this idea of the other could occur only if there was a concept of self to oppose it. Such a distinction was crucial not only for creating images and stereotypes for the racial "other," but equally essential for defining the "self" as the center of unity, power, and civilization. As Frantz Fanon has pointed out in his seminal study *Black Skin, White Masks*, for the white subject, the black other is everything that lies outside the self. For the black subject, however, the white other serves to define everything that is desirable, everything that the self desires. This desire is embedded within a power structure, therefore *"the white man is not only the Other but also the master, real or imaginary"* (138). Portraying the African in most early American plays as a clownish servant, but loyal, faithful, and with a great desire to emulate his white master generally meant that the black character was intended to serve as a mirror against which the *"master culture"* of whites measured themselves and their value systems, thus bolstering their power and cementing their superior status while assuming the inferiority of blacks.[12] The representation of black characters as clownish buffoons reached its peak in popular entertainment with the introduction of minstrel shows. Rice's most popular "Jim Crow" dance and Dan Emmett's unique performances greatly appealed to the largely heterogeneous American audiences of the time which attended minstrel shows and readily applauded what was a rather inaccurate depiction of black culture.[13]

---

[12] During the first quarter of the nineteenth century, the Negro continued to be portrayed as a clownish servant. Then as the Yankee became popular, the Negro character underwent a curious split and was exploited in two ways: in farce or social comedy and in the minstrel show (Meserve 73). See also Moody (32-78).

[13] The impact of minstrel shows' characterization of blacks was so pervasive that permeated a number of American plays. For example, in *Uncle Tom's Cabin*, Topsy's characterization seems to have sprung directly from minstrel shows. For more

According to Jeffrey D. Mason, *"minstrelsy was based more on belief than on fact"* (1993: 116). It displaced the black actuality and created caricatures rather than realistic portrayals of the African-American, which soon evolved into a set of recurring stage types like the Old Uncle and the caring Mammy.[14] Minstrel shows played a crucial part in shaping the white audiences' perception of Blacks and their culture and tradition. As a matter of fact, minstrelsy promoted an image of the African-American as a comic figure, fond of dancing and singing, who, in his simplistic existence, posed no threat to American white society but rather appeared contented and quite harmless. In minstrel shows, the issue of slavery was sufficiently blurred by the persistent cliché of the happy Negro and the highly romanticized, almost idealized, picture of life on Southern plantations. Such representation of slavery was eagerly embraced by the white audiences of the time since it reinforced their own imaginative conception of black people.

In one of the most popular nineteenth-century social comedies, Anna Cora Mowatt's *Fashion* (1845), Zeke, the black character of the play represents the stereotype of the contented, docile black American servant who has so much internalized the values and manners of his white masters that willingly renounces his own identity. Zeke effects his comic part through his eagerness to ape his masters' social conduct.[15] He

---

information on minstrel shows in nineteenth-century American society and popular culture, see Lott, Mahar, and Roediger (115-32).

[14] In 1856, Mrs. Bateman's most successful social comedy *Self*, which seems to have enjoyed a large number of performances both in New York and Boston, introduced Aunt Chloe, the Black Mammy, whose love for Mary, the master's daughter, is so self-effacing that she exclaims:

> *"Now, Miss Ma'y, don't talk dat way 'cept tou want to break your old mammy's heart!*
> *You sit down to teach de pianner, and hear de little gals tum tum, tum, till your head gits most busted? I'll never give my 'sent to you doin' no such thing! I'd rather sell myself to Georgia! Sakes! I'd rather sell myself to the debbil!* "(III, i).

[15] In William Dunlap's *A Trip to Niagara*, produced at the Bowery, Nov. 28, 1828, Job Jerryson, the black character of the play, provides comic relief mainly through his

acquiesces to the devaluation of his own cultural values as he tacitly agrees to change his name to the more fashionable Adolph. So, when, later in the play, Mr. Tiffany calls him Zeke, his reply becomes highly predictable:

> "*Mr. Tif. Zeke.*
> *Zeke. Don't know any such nigga, Boss"* (III, i).

For Zeke, racial identity overrides every other aspect of existence. That is why he strives to adopt *white masks* in the hope that they will somehow make the fact of his blackness vanish. Such schizophrenic existence is grounded in denials— of black history, identity, humanity— a fact that inevitably positions the African-Americans in a perpetual void ultimately questioning their condition in relation to the dominant group.[16]

The dehumanizing aspect of the institution of slavery, that reached deep into the realm of the psyche and the subjectivity of the slaves as well as of their white masters, soon found expression on the American stage with the production of two of the most popular nineteenth-century American plays, George L. Aiken's *Uncle Tom's Cabin* and Dion Boucicault's *The Octoroon.*[17] Written just a few years before the Civil War

---

continuous attempts to emulate the conduct and social manners of the white gentlemen and his persistence in declaring his rights as a freeman.

[16] For Frederick Douglass this denial of the basic human facts of identity is responsible for the African-Americans' oppression and dehumanization:

> "I have no accurate knowledge of my age, never having seen any
> authentic record containing it ..... slaves know as little of their
> age as horses know of their, and it is the wish of most masters .
> to keep their slaves thus ignorant "(1982: 47).

[17] Within a year of the publication of Stowe's novel, there were four versions on the New York stage alone and eleven versions in England. Aiken's play is for the most part remarkably faithful to Stowe's novel and many of the play's lines are taken verbatim from the book. Its success, however, lies in Aiken's ability to achieve melodramatic intensity and sentimental effect through powerful scenes accompanied by music and enhanced by the use of tableaux, such as Eliza's floating across the river on a cake of ice, Little Eva's death, Simon Legree torturing Tom to death, and, of course, the final scene of the play where "*Eva, robed in white, is discovered on the back of a milk-white dove.*" It should be noted that no other American play has had such a remarkable stage history. In the 1850s, productions were seen in London,

and somehow echoing the wider abolitionist sentiments of the ante-bellum American society, the plays signaled a turning point in the theatrical representation of black characters who gained protagonistic status for the first time in the American theatre. Aiken's dramatization of Harriet Beecher Stowe's best-selling novel was first produced at Purdy's National Theatre in New York City on July 18, 1853, and made the unprecedented record of 325 performances. The reaction of the critics of the time to the play's abolitionist sentiments reveals the extent to which the American public was accustomed to a sugar-coated abstraction of slavery than the actuality of black people's oppression. The *New York Herald* (Sept. 3, 1853) pronounced the play's representations of life on the plantations "*most exaggerated enormities of Southern slavery*," while the *Spirit of the Times* (Aug. 6, 1853) clearly disapproved of "*the spirit of this piece, with all its crudities and absurdities.*" But, whatever the contemporary reviewers may have thought of the play, *Uncle Tom's Cabin* made an honest effort at reproducing quite truthfully America's conception of race in the context of racial difference and social division.

Just a few years later, another play, Dion Boucicault's *The Octoroon*, was produced at the Winter Garden Theatre on Dec. 6, 1859, and ran for 48 performances.[18] Boucicault's success as playwright seems to have depended on the fact that he understood quite well the tastes and expectations of his middle-class audiences and created plays that reinforced their values and satisfied their need for gratification. In *The Octoroon*, though he attempts to touch upon such a controversial issue as the institution of slavery, he, nevertheless, preserves class and race lines reassuring his emotionally-charged spectators that the codes of bourgeois respectability and racial purity will eventually emerge intact from chance-ridden circumstances. Viewed against the political and social backdrop of

---

Berlin, and Paris, while some 500 "Tom" companies had been touring the United States by the 1890s. For an account on the stage versions of *Uncle Tom's Cabin*, see Williams (2002: 77-87).

[18] According to Gerald Bordman, "*the play has enjoyed successful revivals, including a fine 1961 mounting by the phoenix Theatre*" (318).

the ante-bellum American society, the plays function as collective affirmations of certain cultural myths and social values. However, although neither *Uncle Tom's Cabin* nor *The Octoroon* can be considered too radical or forcefully outspoken regarding the abolition of slavery, they nevertheless convey a somewhat less self-conscious vision of whiteness and actually move along the gaps and inconsistencies of the American political ideology of the time. To a large extent, the plays represent the "self" and the "other" in terms of a social discourse embedded in contradictions, in the profoundly divisive dialectic of North and South, of antislavery and proslavery, of liberalism and racism.[19] It is precisely these gaps and contradictions that challenge the illusory coherence of the nineteenth-century white, republican culture and expose the plight of those excluded from the democratic vision of American society. Both plays can be read as vehicles of national ideology and cultural debate over the most controversial issue of slavery.

In *Uncle Tom's Cabin* and *The Octoroon* racial ideology seems to arise out of economic exploitation as racial hierarchies depend upon economic and material factors that greatly affect the lives of the slaves as well as their white masters. In both plays, the issue of slavery is closely connected to and actually maintained by economic structures and chance-ridden circumstances which call into question the very humanity of black people, fragment families and eventually destroy the individual,. The precarious finances of the cotton market force the Shelbys to sell Tom, Eliza, and her little son Harry, and the Peytons to lose all their property and have Zoe sold along with the other slaves. As Eliza herself explains in *Uncle Tom's Cabin*:

> "*master don't want to sell, and mistress - she's always good. I*

[19] As Jefferson himself noted of Boucicault's *The Octoroon* , "*the truth of the matter is, it was non-committal. The dialogue and the characters of the play made one feel for the South, but the action proclaimed against slavery and called loudly for its abolition*" (qtd. in Bordman 318).

> *heard her plead and beg for us, but he told her 'twas no use—*
> *that he was in this man's debt, and he had got the power over*
> *him, and that if he did not pay him off clear, it would end in his having to sell the place and all the people and move off* "(I, iii).

In the plays, the economic situation that forces the otherwise *kindly* white masters to unwillingly part with their slaves and which actually betrays the fluid and unstable Southern society and economy is given the mask of evil in the face of Haley and Legree in *Uncle Tom's Cabin* and M'Closky in *The Octoroon*. This way slavery becomes personalized and is treated not as an institution that works within the framework of the entire American culture as part of the integral workings of class and economics, but rather a somewhat localized system based on specific interactions between villain and victims. The reality of slavery as a profitable institution that sustains a capitalist economy is carefully blurred through the introduction of the abstract notion of morality and moral choices that determines black and white personal relations and distinguishes among good and bad white masters. Although the plays attempt to conceal the complex interdependence of economy and the ideology of race underneath the melodramatic mantle of suspenseful circumstances, it nevertheless becomes quite clear that the economic system of the South does not override racial relations but rather intensifies them translating race into social and economic terms:

> "*Marks. How should you like to enter into a nice, profitable business— one that pays well?*
> *Cute. That's just about my measure— it would suit me to a hair. What is it?*
> *Marks. Nigger catching.*
> *Cute. Catching niggers! What on airth do you mean?*

> *Marks. Why, when there's a large reward offered for a runaway darkey, we goes after him, catches him, and gets the reward.*
> *Cute. Yes, that's all right so far— but s'pose there ain't no reward offered?*
> *Marks. Why, then we catches the darkey on our own account, sells him, and pockets the proceeds.*
> *Cute. By chowder, that ain't a bad speculation!*"(*UTC* IV, i).

The social order and the economic structure of the South are not only buttressed by legal sanctions that perpetuate slavery but also depend for their viability upon a hegemonic discourse that instills into the minds of both blacks and whites a belief in the superiority of the white masters and the inferiority of the black slaves. For example, Tom has so much internalized the ideology of race that he cannot even conceive rebelling against the established order of things:

> "*If I must be sold, or all the people on the place, and everything go to rack, why, let me be sold. I s'pose I can bar it as well as anyone. Mas'r always found me on the spot— he always will. I never have broken trust, nor used my pass no ways contrary to my word, and I never will*"(I, iii).

A similar attitude is adopted by Zoe, the sentimental heroine of *The Octoroon*, who in a truly self-effacing manner tells George Peyton "*O, I am nothing; think of yourself*" (II), when financial disaster is about to strike and all the Peyton property, including the slaves, will be put up for sale.

Frantz Fanon, in his analysis of the dehumanizing aspect of colonialism has defined colonized people as not simply those whose labor has been appropriated but those

"*in whose souls an inferiority complex has been created by the death and burial of its local cultural originality*" (18).

This idea becomes intimately connected with the belief that the process of liberation depends upon the African-Americans' ability to define themselves in society and retrieve their culture.[20] The sense of rootlessness, of deprivation of a cultural background, is rather crudely, but no less painfully, expressed by Topsy in Aiken's *Uncle Tom's Cabin*:

> *"Ophelia. Tell me where you was born, and who your father and mother were?*
> *Topsy. Never was born, tell you; never had no father, nor mother, nor nothin'. I was raised by a speculator, with lots of others.*
> *Ophelia. Have you ever heard anything about heaven, Topsy?*
> *[Topsy looks bewildered and grins.] Do you know who made*
> *you?*
> *Topsy. Nobody, as I knows on, he, he, he! I' spect I growed.*
> *Don't think nobody never made me* "(II, ii).

In the opening scene of *The Octoroon*, the grumbling slave Pete says of the black children under his feet:

> "*George. Were they all born on this estate?*
> *Pete. Guess they nebber was born— dem tings! What, dem?— get away! Born here— dem darkies? What, on Terrebonne! Don't b'lieve it, Mas'r George; dem black tings never was born at all*".

---

[20] More than a hundred years later, James Baldwin echoed many of these ideas when he wrote:
"*the truth about a black man, as a historical entity and as a human being, has been hidden from him, deliberately and cruelly; the power of the white world is threatened whenever a black man refuses to accept the white world's definitions*"(1985: 62).

Such remarks echo the Southern logic of fatherlessness and its sustaining system of speculation and exchange. The impression of being adrift and devoid of ancestry proved a powerful method of control, a psychological device to deny the slaves' identity and history, to crush the persistent desire in the slave community to maintain their own sense of culture, and, of course, to deprive them of the possibility to challenge the white world's assumptions and definitions. The prescribed world of the white culture, with its denials, its cruel systems, its imposed silences for the African-Americans who are forced to accept the values and principles of a culture already set out for them is best captured by W.E.B. Du Bois' famous definition of "double consciousness" for the African-American,

> *"always looking at the world through the eyes of others, of measuring one's soul by the tape of a world that looks on in amused contempt and pity"* (215).

This "twoness" of the African-American, who possesses "*two souls, two thoughts, two unreconciled strivings*," takes the form of two essentially antithetical characters in *Uncle Tom's Cabin*, Tom and George Harris (Du Bois 215). Tom's religious nature, which catapults him onto the plane of sainthood, actually frames him into an image of blackness that appears equally appealing and reassuring to the white audiences. Tom has not only unquestioningly and rather pathetically accepted his inferior status in white American society, but has also internalized the most cherished values and ideals of the white culture— piety, morality, honesty. This remarkable combination takes Tom far beyond the stereotypical bestiality and heathenism of the African-American, thus resolving many of the complications that his blackness entails, while his essential passivity as a character divests him of any possibility of rebellion and sexual threat.[21]

[21] It has been argued by a number of scholars that Tom, as a young man, does not really function either socially or sexually. James Baldwin condemns Stowe's novel for presenting an image of Tom that "*has been robbed of his humanity and divested*

Tom is purged of his blackness through his acceptance of the white world view and his ability to wear the *white mask* of the dominant culture. On the other hand, however, George Harris carries a great potential for rebellion and disorder as he represents everything that the white society fears in the African-American. He lacks the discipline and the resignation that Tom exhibits and poses a serious threat to the social order since he openly challenges the immutability of race hierarchies in American society:

> *"George. My master! And who made him my master? That's what I think of! What right has he to me? I'm as much a man as he is!"* (I, i)

The only justification for George's rather disquieting words are a cruel master and the imminent fragmentation of his family. The fact that American blacks have historically been denied the privilege of forming family units in the crucible of race oppression becomes the driving force of George's escape.[22] Later in the play, however, George readily renounces "America," its laws and institutions, as he powerfully exclaims:

> "*My country! What country have I, but the grave? ..... Sir, I haven't any country any more than I have a father. I don't want anything of your country, except to be left alone— to go peaceably out of it; but if any man tries to stop me, let him take care, for I am desperate. I'll fight for my liberty, to the last breath I breathe! You say your*

of his sex" (581), while Elizabeth Ammons describes Tom as a black male version of a sentimental nineteenth-century heroine (172). Moreover, Linda Williams argues for a gender reversal as Tom's passive, feminine traits are sharply juxtaposed to Eliza's "*masculine heroic action*" (62).

[22] In attacking the destruction of families in slavery, American abolitionists posited the family as an instrument of both civilization and character formation. For example, the abolitionist Henry Wright declared that no one who wanted to "*save the world, will overlook the family institution*" (qtd. in Walters 92).

> *fathers did it; if it was right for them, it is right for me!"*(II, iii).[23]

In a paradoxical way, racial and national identities converge at the liminal point where the rhetoric of republicanism transcends the limits of the institution of slavery. Throughout the play, the notion of liberty is contained within the political framework of republican ideology and the post-revolutionary discourse of independence and progress. However, it is particularly interesting to note that despite the obvious emphasis on the value of individual freedom and the necessity of emancipation, the republican promise of all-inclusiveness is exposed in the play as simply an ideological construct, a fabricated national myth. Although the prospect of freedom and equality transforms George Harris into a new man—

> *"Wilson. George, something has brought you out wonderfully. You hold up your head, and move and speak like another man.*
> *George. [Proudly] Because I'm a freeman!"*(II, iii) —

the possibility of escaping his status as a slave, of leaving behind a state of perpetual childhood and finally enter white American society on equal terms, would have been extremely disruptive for the established order of things, that is why George and his family are safely transported to Canada. Furthermore, in the case of Tom, freedom remains in the sphere of imagination and wishful thinking as his dream of eventually becoming a "freeman" never comes true, whereas for Topsy, "liberty" appears to be so

---

[23] The deprivation of any sense of belonging either to a family unit or a whole nation causes the African-Americans to live at the margins of an ideological system that denies them social and political existence. Such a realization is echoed by James Baldwin many years later:
"*It comes as a great shock to discover that the country which is your birthplace and to which you owe your life and identity has not, in the whole system of reality, evolved any place for you* "(1985: 404).

abstract a word that she comically strives to turn it into something more concrete and tangible in order to comprehend its meaning and grasp its reality:

> *"Ophelia. Topsy, I can give you your liberty.*
> *Topsy. My liberty?*
> *Ophelia. Yes, Topsy.*
> *Topsy. Has you got 'um with you?*
> *Ophelia. I have Topsy.*
> *Topsy. Is it clothes or wittles?*
> *Ophelia. How shiftless! Don't you know what your liberty is, Topsy?*
> *Topsy. How should I know when I never seed 'um?"*(IV, iii).

The continuous national effort towards the attainment of the myth of equality, unity and homogeneity is seriously undermined by the new nation's inherent liabilities which stem not so much from the existence of the institution of slavery but the persistence of a racial ideology that determines the limits of the social and cultural acceptance of the "other." The essential contradictions in the political discourse of liberty and equality are primarily the result of the inevitable distance between myth and reality. In the words of St. Claire in *Uncle Tom's Cabin*, the people's common mentality— and hypocrisy— in both the North and the South regarding difference and otherness seems to rise above political principles and expectations:

> "*You would think no harm in a child's caressing a large dog, even if he was black; but a creature that can think, reason and feel, and is immortal, you shudder at. Confess it, cousin. I know the feeling among some of you Northerners well enough. Not that there is a particle of virtue in our not having it,*

> *but custom with us does what Christianity ought to do: obliterates the feeling of personal prejudice. You loathe them as you would a snake or a toad, yet you are indignant at their wrongs. You would not have them abused, but you don't want to have anything to do with them yourselves. Isn't that it?"* (II, ii).

Thus, national identity and its widely advertised values of freedom, equality, and progress become firmly rooted in the uncertain locations of "skin" color or "blood." Far from transcending the confines of a biologized essentialism, the plays inscribe the black/white identity in the body through the identification of corporeality and personhood. Although there is a playful exploration of the identity of the body or the identity that the body represents – demonstrated through racial intermixing, as in the case of Eliza and Zoe— racial and national identity becomes fixed in the body while the body is turned into a sign of an identity that transcends it. This paradox is best exemplified in the character of Zoe whose ambivalent presence in American society raises the question of how the body conveys or contains identity. Obeying the rules of melodrama, Boucicault romanticizes a rather cruel social phenomenon illicitly sanctioned by white American society. By making Zoe an octoroon, the playwright intensifies the tragedy of her situation.[24] As she herself reveals to George Peyton:

> *"Of the blood that feeds my heart, one drop in eight is black— bright red as the rest may be, that one drop poisons all the flood; those seven bright drops give me love like yours— hope like yours— ambition like yours— life hung with passions like dew-drops on the morning flowers; but the one black drop gives me despair, for I am an unclean thing— forbidden by the*

[24] Based on Mayne Reid's novel *The Quadroon* (1856), the play intensifies the pathos of the situation by making Zoe, the heroine, an octoroon. As Richard Moody explains, "*although Zoe retained a noble and romantic spirit, she was distinctly a new addition to the Negro stage-type. Not a servant, she had much of the same status in the household as the whites. Like a typical Southern belle she was gentle, delicate, and frail*" (76).

laws— I'm an Octoroon!"(II).

Zoe's body fails to escape its biological design or destiny and comes to represent a fear that has historically haunted early American society: the fear of *racial pollution*. Despite the constant transgressions of racial boundaries on the southern plantations, the effort to maintain the social purity of the whites remained strong and rooted deeply into the ideology of absolute racial difference. Miscegenation was a nightmare since race functioned as the most powerful and yet the most fragile marker of human identity. The instability of "race" as a category is suggested in the play through the possibility of racial mixing, or to use one of the most widely employed and most disputed terms in post-colonial theory, "hybridity."[25] Zoe, as a "hybrid" species, however, somehow subverts Homi K. Bhabha's definition of

"a cultural hybridity that entertains difference without an assumed or imposed hierarchy" as she represents not just the liminal space of racial interchange but rather establishes the polarities and inequalities of racial relations" (Bhabha 1994: 4).

As an octoroon, Zoe's presence in American society is essentially problematic. Almost white in skin-color, manners, and language, Zoe is still considered black and a slave, a "*poisoned thing*" (II) as she calls herself, whose biological and social existence bears the characteristics and discontinuities of two races. She inhabits a zone of ambivalence in American society that grants her neither identity nor difference. Zoe's "split subjectivity," to borrow the term from Lacan, springs from her own feelings of psychic dislocation as she is, on the one hand, invited to move within the dominant white world, while, on the other, she is marginalized by the same culture she was brought up to revere and emulate:

---

[25] The term "hybridity" has been most recently associated with the work of Homi K. Bhabha, whose analysis of colonizer/colonized relations stresses their interdependence and the mutual construction of their subjectivities. The use of the term, however, has been widely criticized since it usually implies negating and neglecting the imbalance and inequality of he power relations it references.

> *"George. We can leave this country, and go far away where none can know.*
> *Zoe. And your mother, she who from infancy treated me with*
> *such fondness, she who, as you said, has most reason to spurn me can she forget what I am? Will she gladly see you wedded to the child of her husband's slave? No! she would revolt from it, as all but you would. And if I consented to hear the cries of my heart, if I did not crush out my infant love, what would she say to the poor girl on whom she had bestowed so much? No, no!*
> *George. Zoe, must we immolate our lives on her prejudice?*
> *Zoe. Yes, for I'd rather be black than ungrateful! Ah, George,*
> *our race has at least one virtue— it knows how to suffer!"*(II).

Zoe becomes at once resemblance and menace. She in fact possesses a flawed identity as she is obliged to mirror back an image of whiteness but in imperfect form, almost the same but not quite. Zoe becomes the embodiment of symbolic ambiguity and contradictory notions of racial identity— white or black? But she employs this ambiguity not to subvert the authority of the white culture but rather to enhance it. Although she challenges race hierarchies momentarily through her love for George Peyton, her death at the end of the play leaves the social order intact from any kind of racial mixing, thus reassuring the American audiences of the immutability of racial categories:

> *"George. O, Zoe! What have you done?*
> *Zoe. Last night I overheard you weeping' in your room, and you said, 'I'd rather see her dead than so!'*

> *George. Have I then prompted you to this?*
> *Zoe. No; but I loved you so, I could not bear my fate; and then I stood between your heart and hers. When I am dead she will not be jealous of your love foe me, no laws will stand between us*" (V, iv).

Throughout *The Octoroon*, as well as *Uncle Tom's Cabin*, race remains the currency of interaction and the primal factor in defining the discourse of human relations. No matter what the main characters' allotted destinies may be— George's recolonization in Canada, Tom's redemption, Zoe's death— their racial identities determine their status as individuals and as interactive members of American society. The sentimental foundation of both plays makes their critique of slavery rather vulnerable. Obeying the imperative of melodrama for the restoration of the moral and social order and the demand to satisfy the feelings and expectations of the audience, the plays eventually confirm the fundamental racism of the American society. *The Octoroon* and *Uncle Tom's Cabin* personalize slavery and racism and actually avoid clear-cut definitions and solutions, thus tacitly ensuring the endurance of racial hierarchies and leaving the American society uncensured and the white audiences' guilt expiated.

WORKS CITED

Ammons, Elizabeth. "Heroines in *Uncle Tom's Cabin.*" *American Literature* 49 (1977): 161-79.

Baldwin, James. *The Price of the Ticket: Collected Essays 1948-85.* London: Michael Joseph, 1985.

____________. "Everybody's Protest Novel." *Partisan Review* 16 (1949) : 578-85.

Bercovitch, Sacvan. *The Rites of Assent: Transformations in the Symbolic Construction of America.* New York: Routledge, 1993.

Bhabha, Homi K. *The Location of Culture.* London: Routledge, 1994.

Bordman, Gerald. *The Concise Oxford Companion to American Theatre.* New York: Oxford UP, 1987.

Brooks, Peter. *The Melodramatic Imagination.* New York: Columbia UP, 1984.

Burstein, Andrew. *Sentimental Democracy: The Evolution of America's Romantic Self-Image.* New York: Hill, 1999.

Dillon, Merton L. *The Abolitionists: The Growth of a Dissenting Minority.* DeKalb: Northern Illinois UP, 1974.

Douglass, Frederick, "The Meaning of July Fourth for the Negro," Speech at Rochester, New York, July 5, 1852." *The Life and Writings of Frederick Douglass* vol. 2. Ed. Philip S. Foner. New York: International, 1950.

___________ . *The Narrative of the Life of Frederick Douglass, An American Slave.* Harmondsworth: Penguin, 1982.

DuBois, W.E.B. *The Souls of Black Folks, in Three Negro Classics.* New York: Avon, 1965.

Fanon, Frantz. *Black Skin, White Masks.* Trans. C. L. Markmann. New York: Grove, 1967.

Foner, Eric. *Free Soil, Free Labor, Free Men: The Ideology of the Republican Party before the Civil War.* New York: Oxford, 1970.

Gramsci, Antonio. *Selections from the Prison Notebooks of Antonio Gramsci.* Ed. Quintin Hoare and Geoffrey Nowell-Smith. New York: International, 1971.

Hays, Michael and Anastasia Nikolopoulou, eds. *Melodrama: The Cultural Emergence of a Genre.* New York: St. Martin's, 1996.

Levine, Lawrence W. *Highbrow/Lowbrow: The Emergence of Cultural Hierarchy in America.* Cambridge, Mass.: Harvard UP, 1988.

Lott, Eric. Love and Theft: Blackface Minstrelsy and the American Working-Class. New York: Oxford UP, 1993.

McConachie, Bruce A. *Melodramatic Formations: American Theatre and Society, 1820-1870.* Iowa: U of Iowa P, 1992.

Mahar, William J. *Behind the Burnt Cork Mask: Early Blackface Minstrelsy and Antebellum American Popular Culture.* Urbana: U of Illinois P, 1999.

Mason, Jeffrey D. and J. Ellen Gainor, eds. *Performing America: Cultural Nationalism in American Theatre.* Ann Arbor: The U of Michigan P, 1999.

_____________. *Melodrama and the Myth of America.* Bloomington: Indiana UP, 1993.

Matthews, Jean V. *Toward A New Society: American Thought and Culture, 1800-1830.* Boston: Twayne, 1991.

Miles, R. *Racism.* London: Routledge, 1989.

Moody, Richard. *America Takes the Stage: Romanticism in American Drama and Theatre, 1750-1900.* Millwood, N.Y.: Kraus, 1977.

Meserve, Walter J. *An Outline History of American Drama.* New York. Prospero, 1994.

Pease, Donald E. *National Identities and Post-Americanist Narratives.* Durham: Duke UP, 1994.

Powell, Timothy B. *Ruthless Democracy: A Multicultural Interpretation of the American Renaissance.* Princeton: Princeton UP, 2000.

Richards, Leonard L. *"Gentlemen of Property and Standing" : Anti-Abolition Mobs in Jacksonian America.* New York: Oxford UP, 1970.

Roediger, David R. *The Wages of Whiteness: Race and the Making of the American Working Class.* New York: Verso, 1991.

Shalhope, Robert E. *The Roots of Democracy: American Thought and Culture, 1760-1800.* Boston: Twayne, 1990.

Tocqueville, Alexis de. *Democracy in America.* Ed. J.P. Mayer. New York: Harper Perennial, 1988.

Walters, Ronald. *The Anti-Slavery Appeal: American Abolitionism after 1830.* Baltimore: John Hopkins, 1976.

Williams, Linda. *Playing the Race Card: Melodramas of Black and White from Uncle Tom to O.J. Simpson.* Princeton, N.J.: Princeton UP, 2002.

Williams, Raymond. "Base and Superstructure in Marxist Cultural Theory."*Rethinking Popular Culture: Contemporary Perspectives in Cultural Studies.* Ed. Chandra Mukerji and Michael Schudson. Berkeley: U of California P, 1991. 407-23.

III.2 Csaba Csapó: Ideology behind the Aesthetic: The Relationship between Language Use, Political Correctness and Sexual Harassment in *Oleanna* by David Mamet

As a result of the prominence of postmodern and post-structuralist discourses on art and culture, it seems that Cultural Studies has dominated over literary criticism and aesthetics by the end of the twentieth century. Following Arthur C. Danto freely (*mutatis mutandis*), it would be worth taking a closer look at the question of what led to the disfranchisement of literary criticism by Cultural Studies.[1] Cultural Studies, which includes various postmodern and post-structuralist theories, approaches art as only one of many various sectors of cultural activity, and thus the most recent tendencies in literary criticism seem to forget to say something about the aesthetic value of the literary text. Yet it seems, after some recent publications of Theodor Adorno[2], Frederic Jameson[3], and *The New Aestheticism*[4], it is becoming evident that the question of aesthetics will have to be reassessed once again. "old-fashioned" terms such as "literary value," "beauty," and "aesthetics" seem to be regaining currency after being virtually discredited in analyses which made political power, institution, and ideology the focus of their conceptual apparatus. Instead of a complacent discourse about the verities of former aesthetic theories, new aestheticism presents a fundamental challenge to old-style aesthetics. In the introductory passage of *New Aestheticism,* John J. Joughin and Simon Malpas claim:

---

[1] See Arthur C. Danto. *The Philosophical Disenfranchisement of Art.* New York: Columbia University Press, 1986.

[2] Theodor Adorno. *Aesthetic Theory*, ed. Tr. And intro. By Robert Hullot-Kentor, Minneapolis: University of Minnesota Press, 1997.

[3] Frederic Jameson. *A Singular Modernity: Essays on the Ontology of the Present.* London: Verso, 2002.

"Art is inextricably tied to the politics of contemporary culture, and has been throughout modernity. Aesthetic specificity is not, however, entirely explicable, or graspable, in terms of another conceptual scheme or genre or discourse. The singularity of the work's 'art-ness' escapes and all that often remains is the critical discourse itself, reassured of its methodological approach and able to reassert its foundational principles. In other words, perhaps the most basic tenet that we are trying to argue for is the equiprimordiality of the aesthetic— that, although it is without doubt imbricated with the political, historical, ideological, etc., thinking it as other than determined by them, and therefore reducible to them, opens a space for an artistic or literary specificity that can radically transform its critical potential and position with regard to contemporary culture. In the light of this, we want to put the case that it might be time for a new aestheticism" (Joughin, Malpas 2003).

The polarization into "materialist," i.e. "politically charged" ideology of aesthetics and the "formalist" one seems insufficient to see the complexity of the question about how art works. The problematic of this polarization has already been explored thoroughly in Adorno's *Aesthetic Theory*. What New Aestheticism suggests is a major challenge to open a more reflective phase in criticism irreducible to the exclusive political, historical and ideological commitments of contemporary society and to understand the truth-potential of art in its unique "art-ness." In my paper I do not intend to discuss deeply the above-mentioned problems; rather I aim at pointing out that certain literary texts, in this case David Mamet's drama, limit, or even resist the interpretation when regarding it only as to what extent literary forms and conventions can be identified as (natural) manifestations of specific ideologemes or even as determining formats of particular ideological discourses.

From the 1990s, political correctness and sexual harassment became important issues in American culture. The Clinton vs. Lewinski

---

[4] John J. Joughin & Simon Malpas, eds. *The New Aestheticism*. Manchester: Manchester University Press, 2003.

case with all its negative and ridiculous aspects put our concepts about sexual harassment in a new light. David Mamet's *Oleanna* is a thought-provoking play that looks at the issue of sexual harassment on-campus in a radical light. The issue of sexual harassment is posited into the context of political correctness and concerns the relationship between language use, power and gender relations. Since the New York premiere of *Oleanna* on October 25, 1992, drama and literary critics alike have been eagerly analyzing the play in search of both authorial intention and a concrete definition of the work's ideology. Actually, critics of the play have reached a number of very different but collectively plausible ideas. Many feminist critics claim that *Oleanna* is a misogynist drama, an overt attack against feminism; some other critics have pointed out the importance of the phenomenological blind spots, that of the extra-scenic "characters" such as John's wife, the Tenure Committee, or Carol's group. Most of the critics agree in regarding the text as a complex net of Foucauldian power structures. Although Foucault's theory on power relations in society is invoked within this play on one level, my intention in this essay is to point out that on another level, the above mentioned Foulcauldian theorization serves as a means to make John and Carol equal representatives of a certain condition rather than feuding representatives of gender, power, violence, or any other currently hypothesized duality. In this view, it seems, the binary oppositions within the ideological and political background outside the play collapse. It seems that the text itself resists a univocal reading of the ideologies behind it.

Personally, I cannot agree with the feminist critics who anathematized Mamet for *Oleanna*; the play is not any kind of attack against feminism as they claim but rather more complex than one could typify it with the binary opposition of feminist/anti-feminist. In my view, if one tries to understand the drama only from the basis of power relations and concentrates only on the underlying ideologies, he/she will lose the aesthetic value of it. *Oleanna* is neither a thesis, nor an anti-thesis drama since Mamet does not take sides for or against one or the other political, ideological trend. The dramatist presents a considerably multi-layered theme in *Oleanna*; it challenges spectators/readers to step aside from their own preconceived ideologically based notions of what contemporary American culture defines as "sexual harassment" and "political correctness." The play gives a highly balanced perspective and examines these issues from a complex point of view of communication and language use, which is rather personal and intimate.

In *Act One*, Carol, a college student, goes to her professor, John, to discuss why she failed his course, while he is having a long, private telephone conversation, keeping the girl waiting. John's explanation of worry that Carol is a bright girl who performs poorly in class is punctuated with phone calls from the professor's wife and a friend, during which they discuss John's purchase of a new house and his upcoming hearing at the tenure committee. Carol tells John that she is worried about her grades, but she also wishes to understand what he teaches; she simply cannot understand anything that is going on in class. Carol says she feels stupid and she had always been taught to feel stupid. John sympathizes with this feeling; he opens up and tells Carol that he had also been brought up to feel stupid; furthermore, he takes the blame for Carol's lack of understanding in his class and proposes that they should start the whole course from the beginning, in his office room. John's idea is that during their private lessons his task, as a teacher, will be to provoke Carol mentally. Then the telephone rings again and from John's and his wife's conversation Carol figures out that John's buying a new house is somehow connected with his tenure at college. John connects the situation of his possible tenure to Carol's problem suggesting that tests, like those of the tenure committee, which has announced but not yet approved him, are meaningless; he also claims that the tests students have to take are meaningless in the same way. According to him, the structure of higher education is mostly artificial, and the established teacher-student relationship is not necessary or important. John wonders why Carol wants to get a degree at all; the girl contradicts him arguing that she has the right to higher education. Carol misunderstands what his professor speaks about, or rather, she interprets it in a different way and she becomes frustrated. She interprets John's action that he wants to fool her in the same way, as he had fooled his wife on the telephone. When John whips the system of higher education, Carol *asks "...if education is so bad, why do you do it?"* [5] John's answer is nothing but a platitude*: "I do it because I love it"* (35). John goes up to her because he wants to comfort her physically, but the girl walk away. Two misunderstandings happen at the same time: one on the mental, and one on the physical level.

As Act Two opens, Carol has filed a complaint with the tenure committee regarding John. He feels guilty because of his own self-concern and selfish desire for tenure, but he ultimately feels her charges are exaggerated. The charges say he is sexist, elitist, racist, was alone with her, moved to physically embrace her, told her a sexually explicit story, and offered her grades in exchange for private visits to his office. She tells him that he is powerless to deny the actions, but he is steadfast that she is wrong in her charges and that he wishes to help her. Carol mentions that she has consulted on this matter with her "Group," and they cannot withdraw the complaint. John wants to talk to Carol, but she tells him the proper venue for these discussions is at the hearing of the tenure committee. The girl turns to go, but John physically restrains her saying he just wants to talk to her; the act ends with Carol's call for help.

By the third act, John has lost his job and, at the same time, his social security. Carol insists that the charges are absolute facts and takes her charges very seriously; she claims that John's sexism is not only against her but also against the female gender. Then she says she desires not revenge but understanding. John is insistent in attempting to discover how he may end Carol's attacks, and she ultimately offers a bargain; she and her "group" are willing to withdraw their charges if John recommends the banning of certain books at the college and signs a statement of support. John refuses to do so when the telephone rings again. It is Jerry, John's friend, advising him that Carol and her group are

[5] David Mamet. *Oleanna*. New York : Pantheon Books, 1992.

considering pursuing criminal charges against John for battery and attempted rape. Carol argues that, in her view, John's behavior was rape:

"'I saw you, Professor. For two semesters sit here, stand there and exploit our, as you thought, 'paternal prerogative,' and what is that but rape; I swear to God'" (66-67).

John's wife telephones again and he asks Carol to leave. As she leaves the room, she warns John that he should not dare to call his wife "baby." John knocks Carol down, begins to beat her. JOHN: *"You vicious little bitch. You think you can come in here with your political correctness and destroy my life?"* (79) Then John picks up a chair, raises it above his head, and advances on her. *JOHN: "You little cunt!"* (79) He looks down at her, lowers the chair, goes to his desk and arranges some papers on it. The replication to John's last word comes from Carol: *"Yes. That's right. Yes. That's right"* (80).

The basic dramatic situation in *Oleanna* comes from an exaggerated manifestation of political correctness. The other obvious source of conflict in the drama is the communication or miscommunication, or, rather, the breakdown of communication between the two characters; between the man and the woman, between the ones belonging to the higher and the lower social class, between the older and the younger as well as between the more conservative and the more progressive ones. These two sources of tension are actually only one, because Mamet posits the theme of sexual harassment in the context of language use. From the works of feminist linguists, it is well-known that language and gender are closely related to each other; many scholars have pointed out the ways in which language works to maintain (and potentially transform) hierarchical gender arrangements and ideologies. Most power struggles ultimately end up finding their base in the way two people speak to each other. *Oleanna* is very difficult to read; the language of the play is minimalist, abundant in clipped and always interrupted dialogues, and the sentences are rather short and elliptical. The characters often tear the word out of each other's mouths, not even being interested what the other person is going to say. Carol's first sentence in the play is a question: *"What is a 'term of art'?"* (2) John says after a pause: *"I'm sorry…?"* (2) Then Carol repeats her question. The very first replication between the characters imply that the communication is impossible between them.

The form of the dialogue often expresses otherwise hidden characteristics of the speaker. At the beginning of the play, John does most of the talking and most of the interrupting, showing his dominance over Carol in conversation and his comfort in his role as lecturer. He speaks almost exclusively and does not place importance on the other person in the conversation. He fills his speech with overtly elaborate words and academic allusions, for which Carol constantly asks clarification. Only few sentences are completed, and the characters' speech constantly overlaps. In *Act Two*, both characters speak more freely; Carol expresses her points, and John only quiets her with a long, rambling speech reminiscent of *Act One*. In *Act Three,* Carol assumes John's original role constantly interrupting him and not really listening to what he says. His expression is limited because of Carol's power role, and thus true communication never occurs.

Carol's behavior and actions are rather simple but her character is all the more complicated and consequently enigmatic. In *Act One*, she is the naïve female student, who, on the one hand, is interested in her final grade; on the other hand, she did not really come to college because of pursuit of knowledge but because she would like to get a degree in order to have better working and life opportunities. However, she feels desperate because of her scholastic failure, and all this leads her to self-hatred. By the end of the play, her character develops to a great deal; she becomes an intelligent, manipulative woman with a strongly developed political agenda. The background of this great development of Carol's is a phenomenological blind spot of drama. Subtle clues such as her involvement with a group of advisers and her extensive knowledge in the university and legal statutes regarding harassment are not developed and elaborated; nevertheless, they are pivotal to the plot. What motivates Carol to undergo such a change can have two equally difficult interpretations. One can regard her as the manipulator who has constructed a naïve facade during previous interactions with John. Also, one can think of her character as going through an incredible progression with very little obvious motivation, be it external influence or, as she describes, the simple troubles of someone of her socio-economic background. In this case, it seems she has found a means of politically-ideologically based power to compensate her frustrations or work off her aggression deriving from her scholastic and womanly failure. Yet Carol's motivation seems to be a mystery to the reader/spectator.

In contrast to Carol's secretive nature, John is an open and honest character; he shares his motivations with the reader/spectator, and he speaks freely about his passions and desires. It would be rather a mere simplification to analyze his character as an unmistakable representative of the oppressive white male elite who may even sexually harass female students. He is rather honest in his confusion, exasperation, desperation, and ultimate denial. Another misreading of this character would be if one thought that he is a positive hero who is empathic and progressive in his views, a victim of feminism. The play starts with a girl student waiting anxiously for her professor to discuss her final grade, while the professor is having a long telephone conversation about his private matters. His behavior suggests as if he overrode his student. His conversation with Carol is overbearing, he relentlessly interrupts her and often does not respond to what she actually says talking instead on a topic important to him. His use of academic expressions and his frequent allusions characterize him as both well educated and perhaps haughty, and Carol certainly seems to think that he overuses big words in an attempt to belittle her. He begins the play repeatedly interrupting Carol, which shows his lack of concern for her right of speech and his own self-esteem. Similarly, when, in *Act Three,* Carol begins interrupting John, she recognizes and takes advantage of her own power over him which allows her to show disregard for his rights. John, in *Act One*, does not even realize how he humiliates Carol with his claiming that her term paper is not worth a bean, then he tears off her paper, and finally he suggests that they start the course again from the beginning. He is always whipping the system of higher education, although he gains his social status and power from that system. He questions the necessity of a college education; for him, college is a ritualized form of "hazing," in which teachers go through the traditional motions, claiming that they teach while really inculcating the students with the belief that higher education is good and necessary.

Carol, however, takes this as an assault upon her right to an education, arguing that she and other students come from a much lower social status than John, and their families make a lot of financial effort in order that their children can learn. She says they work very hard and people like John, make it more difficult for those students to learn because of their power roles. A valid question arises in *Oleanna* concerning education: Is the entire institution of higher education in the United States hopelessly patriarchal— the province of white men of privilege, who wield academic power for the intent purpose of continuing to suppress, subjugate and sexually harass female student? If not— and it seems that in fact, it is not— then how is it possible that the behavior and language use of certain professors can be misunderstood? Modern analytic philosophy points out how logical paradoxes, which produce a self-contradiction by accepted ways of reasoning, occur (e.g. Eubulides' famous liar-paradox, according to which Epimenides, a Cretan, says that all Cretans are liars). If two or more abstraction levels of the language are mixed up within the same system, this leads to paradoxes. *Per analogiam*, John's ideas and intentions are misunderstood by Carol because he mistakes his role; on the one hand, he blurs up different levels of communication, he does not keep the distinction between the public and the private sphere. He makes the mistakes— although unintentionally— with his involving the student in his private life, while she, the student, came for official reason. Sometimes he communicates with Carol as a friend, sometimes as her professor. Later, when he speaks about his views on higher education to Carol, he overestimates her status and treats the girl as if she had a higher status than one she holds; he does not recognize the fact that Carol is his student, not his colleague.

The relationship between John and Carol is influenced by outer phenomena as well. The ringing of the telephone signals the invisible presence of power. It seems that communication in the play is more important structurally than textually; the ringing phone ranges in role from having a function of an interruption in John's convincing rhetoric to a sort of *deus ex machina* which controls the lives of the characters on stage. John's interruptions reveal much of his character, and the clipped conversations suggest that the characters are not able to understand each other. When the phone rings, it is always John's call, and only he is shown to communicate with someone else. Carol mentions a group of advisers several times but there is no evidence that they exist or how she communicates with them. The other dramaturgical role of the telephone is to permeate the slow and sullen dialogue between John and Carol; when there is a hope for real communication between them, ringing of the telephone arrests the dialogue. The intrusion of the external world into the conflict between John and Carol illustrates how the social context fashions both characters' lives. This is not very new in the history of drama; in *Intrigue and Love* by Friedrich Schiller, the source of the tragedy is that the Miller family think they can prevent their daughter, Luise, from the outer, corrupt "world of intrigue," but, finally, as it turns out, they cannot, because the "world of intrigue" has become part of the social context in which they live. Whereas in *Intrigue and Love* the problem is that the corrupt outer world destroys the lives of honorable families, in *Oleanna* both Carol and John came to a turning point in their lives where their social security is at stake.

Mamet gives very few staging directions in *Oleanna*; there are no references in the text how the scene of action looks, what the dimensions of John's room are, there are no stage directions concerning the lightening, costumes, make-up, etc. There are no allusions whether Carol tempts John sexually. In case of a theatrical production of this play for a spectator, or otherwise for a reader, the play offers many empty spaces to be interpreted. To understand Mamet, however, one must realize that his dramaturgical approach is to challenge the spectator/reader as well as the actors with such unresolved lacunae. In *American Drama since 1960*, Matthew C. Roudané gives an excellent analysis of what I call a series of "gaps" in the realistic veneer, which should be used as the basis for any analysis of *Oleanna*:

"Mamet returns to a world in which the gaps between words and deeds remain. The play is theatrically powerful precisely because its author never fills in such gaps. Instead, the theatergoer thinks, Is Carol framing John? Are her accusations legitimate? Is Carol simply the first to have the courage to challenge a patronizing and, perhaps, womanizing male teacher? Is John so much a part of an inherently misogynistic world that he is blithely unaware that his well-meaning actions are in fact highly sexist? Mamet invites the audience to respond to these and many other issues [...]" (Roudané 1960: 173).

The play provides a brilliant illustration of how projective identification can be deployed by a would-be victim to create a situation that she will later be able to label as "sexual harassment." *Oleanna* has many things in common with *Miss Julie* by August Strindberg; both plays were criticized by feminists because of their alledged misogyny and anti-feminism. As in *Miss Julie* both Jean and Julie are oppressors and victims, sadists and masochists at the same time, also in *Oleanna* both characters are victims, and neither of them is any better than the other. Carol's response to John's last words ("JOHN: You little *cunt*! CAROL: *Yes. That' right."*) is not unequivocal either; one can think that Carol has succumbed to John's "male arrogance" and has accepted her subdued gender position; or her last words may suggest that she has become a victim of her "group," i.e. she has not become an emancipated woman but only a means of a harsh feminist group.

Another interesting question to consider is why most spectators, readers and critics think that Carol became influenced by a feminist group; she mentions "her group" but a spectator/reader does not know anything about this group, not even whether there exists any advising group behind Carol's actions. In my view, the spectator/reader may easily fall into the trap of interpreting the play— either as pro- or anti-feminist— based on the political-or ideological background. This trap is hardly to be seen since the play teems with the allusions to contemporary cultural and critical theories embedded in the verbal action that influences the plot essentially. Ideology is an important element in the play, but it seems that the dramaturgy of *Oleanna* is manipulated in such a way by this contextual reading that the reader is pushed into a dichotomy of agreement or disagreement with who is to blame. While at the first glance this play seems to be realistic, actually it is not since it investigates hidden ideological assumptions of realism that is intertwined with power relations.

The mention of power would then call to mind "power-theorist" Michel Foucault who postulates that power is a discourse that exists prior to institutions and social relations. According to him, power belongs to no one but is used by everyone. Knowledge is power and this is what John readily employs to "subdue" his student. Claiming power by being a dissenter from the educational system that breeds an emphasis on grades as the measure of success, John tries to remind Carol that the purpose of a college education is the love for learning. Ironically, he succumbs to the discourse of academia and frustrates a somewhat bewildered Carol who chooses to note down phrases in abstract and later concocts a new narrative of her encounters with the professor to the school's disciplinary board. The power balance is shifted from the beginning to the end through the use of a three-act structure. In the final act, it is Carol who, through an unanticipated eloquence, is lecturing the professor now standing accused of being a megalomaniac that preys on the ignorant and unenlightened, demonstrating that power belongs to the one who controls the discourse of speech.

Did John "sexually harass" Carol with his seemingly sexist and derogatory remarks or was Carol misinterpreting his intentions and re-interpreting them in the light of her own insecurities? What constitutes sexual harassment or rape? In *Oleanna*, I believe these issues can encourage the audience to misinterpret the play; the themes of political correctness and sexual harassment easily lead the process of interpretation to the hermeneutics of suspicion. This term was coined by the French philosopher Paul Ricoeur in the 1970s for a method of interpretation which assumes that the literal or surface-level meaning of a text is an effort to conceal the political interests which are served by the text. The purpose of interpretation using hermeneutics of suspicion is to strip off the concealment, unmasking those interests. It seems that the attempts to interpret interesting political and ideological questions raised in *Oleanna* by the standards of any ideologically based critical tools can lead only to frustration. The play itself is a provocative one since it opens questions to think over. What seems to be rather ironic, however, is that the question of ideology within the play, represented by the language use, class, gender, power relations, resists an only ideologically based interpretation.

WORKS CITED

Adorno, Theodor. *Aesthetic Theory*. Ed. tr. and intro. by Robert Hullot-Kentor. Minneapolis: University of Minnesota Press, 1997.

Danto, Arthur, C. *The Philosophical Disenfranchisement of Art*. New York: Columbia UP, 1986.

Jameson, Frederick. *A Singular Modernity: Essays on the Ontology of the Present*. London: Verso, 2002.

Joughin, John, J. and Malpas, Simon. eds. *The New Aestheticism*. Manchester: Manchester University Press, 2003.

Mamet, David. *Oleanna*. New York : Pantheon Books, 1992.

Roudané, Matthew, C. *American Drama Since 1960: A Critical History*. New York: Twayne, 1996.

III.3 Wojciech Kallas: Us and Them: The Ambivalence of Ideology in Public Enemy's Rap Songs

Rap music seems to be perfectly suited for analysis since it represents much more than mere entertainment and serves an important social function. In the African-American community music has traditionally voiced resistance to oppression and rap is a form of music which developed in the new urban environment inhabited by blacks in the USA[1]. Chuck D, the leader of *Public Enemy*, suggests that rap is *"the CNN of the African-American community."*[2]

In fact, rap concerts very often inform the members of the black community in the USA about the most important developments concerning black Americans. This chapter analyses the lyrics of the song *Louder than a Bomb* by the famous rap group *Public Enemy*. The piece comes from their 1991 album *It Takes a Nation of Million to Hold Us Back*. I intend to show how this song challenges stereotypical images of blacks. I argue that many of these representations constructed the "other" on the basis of white racist ideology created to keep blacks in inferior positions. The paper demonstrates how *Public Enemy* advocates an alternative "black" ideology, referring to the ideas put forward in his speeches by Malcolm X as well as to other theories of "black" identity.

The very name of the group— *Public Enemy*— suggests a conflict with the mainstream American society and threat to the (white) establishment. The very concept of "enemy," however, seems to be ambiguous. It was the white man that created the "enemy." The "enemy" was constructed in order to justify colonisation. The ideology of racism was a useful tool in the process of legitimising exploitation, it was a discourse of power based on binary oppositions which favours certain forms of identity and marginalises others. In medieval Europe, colour symbolism was clear: "white" meant "goodness" and "black" meant "evil."

[1] Douglas Kellner, *Media Culture: Cultural Studies, Identity and Politics between the Modern and the Postmodern* (London and New York: Routledge, 1998), p. 174.

The black skin of Africans was believed to mirror and represent the polluted soul of its owner. The negative associations of "blackness" were readily used by the white man to differentiate between the fair-skinned people and "blacks." The term comprised all Africans despite the varying degrees of darkness of their skin complexion and in time it was further extended to include all non-white peoples, which thus proves that the division was a mere political construction and not a straightforward representation of difference.[3] The ideology of racism shows striking affinities with the colonial discourse as analysed by Jan Mohamed, who argues that

> *"All the evil characteristics and habits with which the colonialist endows the native are [...] not presented as products of social and cultural difference but as characteristics inherent in the race— in the "blood"—of the native."*[4]

Therefore, it seems that the white elite chose to create an "enemy" in order to justify conquest, slavery and later the ideology of white racial superiority.

The name of the rap band *Public Enemy* clearly refers to and deconstructs this image of the "black enemy." The word "public" suggests that the "enemy" is the foe of the mainstream society, and thus only a minority. It also emphasises the outsider status of the black community in the USA. In fact, many songs by *Public Enemy* enumerate instances of mistreatment by the (white) authorities. In a line from the song *Louder than a Bomb*: *"I'll never be a friend / Of those with closed minds",* Chuck D reveals his awareness of the fact that it is the white majority that has been

---

[2] Kellner, *Media Culture,* p. 180.

[3] Cf. Errol Lawrence, "In the Abundance of Water the Fool Is Thirsty: Sociology and Black 'Pathology'," in: *The Empire Strikes Back: Race and Racism in 70s Britain*. ed. P. Gilroy. London and New York: Routledge, 1994, pp. 59-60.

[4] Abdul R. JanMohamed, "The Economy of Manichean Allegory," in: *The Post-colonial Studies Reader*. ed. B. Ashcroft et al. London and New York: Routledge, 1999, pp. 20-21.

responsible for creating an enemy out of the African-American community.

The name of the leader of *Public Enemy* seems to be an equally significant element in the deconstruction of the white dominant ideology of racism. He adopted the name Chuck D, which is significant for several reasons. As Kellner suggests,

"rap artists often utilise a pseudonym [...] to signify either the anonymity of black voices, or the need to take on another persona to express their concerns. The name serves as a mask in the tradition of African culture and signifies, on some occasions, that the rapper is speaking for the group, or community, as well as themselves."[5]

Clearly, Chuck D speaks on behalf of (part of) the black community as he refers to many important problems plaguing his fellow people. Moreover, Chuck D's decision seems to refer to the example set by Malcolm X who changed his name for "X." The new name was supposed to symbolise his true, lost (African) name and by doing so Malcolm X rejected the identity forced on him by the white man.[6]

Public Enemy's song *Louder than a Bomb* conveys deep dissatisfaction with the position of blacks in the USA and shows distrust towards the white establishment. Like Malcolm X, *Public Enemy* claim that those are the (white) authorities that are to blame for the degradation of the African-American community. The lyrics clearly suggest that the rappers and, supposedly, their African-American audience are aware of the methods used by the dominant white discourse invented to keep blacks in inferior position. The message springing from Chuck D's appeal "leave alone the grown" becomes crystal-clear if we analyse the language used by Uncle Sam in dealing with other minority groups:

---

[5] Kellner, *Media Culture*, p. 178.

[6] Lawrence H. Fuchs, *The American Kaleidoscope: Race, Ethnicity, and the Civic Culture*, p. 179.

"Say to my Choctaw children, and my Chickasaw children to listen— my white children of Mississippi have extended their law over their country[...]Where they now are, say to them, their father cannot prevent them from being subject to the laws of the State of Mississippi[...] Say to the chiefs and warriors that I am their friend, that I wish to act as their friend but they must[...]by being settled on the lands I offer them, put it in my power to be such— There, beyond of the limits of any State, in possession of land of their own, which they shall posses as long as Grass grows or water runs. I am and will protect them and be their friend and father".[7]

The suggestion that black (Indian, Filipino, etc.) people could not take care of themselves, because they were only children, legitimised white domination in the past. The image of the father was particularly useful for conquest because it also suggests that the loving parent does what is best for the children, even if they do not appreciate or understand his actions. The lyrics of the song analysed here reveal the paternalistic ideology hidden behind such assumptions and inform us that essentially the same tactic is still used in relation to the African-American community. Malcolm X in one of his speeches noticed that *"[i]n this country the black can be fifty years old and he is still a "boy".*[8] The song implies that "children" are not able to solve their problems themselves and the white authorities have to do it for them.

Louder than a Bomb makes other references to the white paternalistic ideology. When Chuck D warns "*Wait before you treat me like a stepchild,"* he states clearly that Uncle Sam has never treated his "children" properly. The term "stepchild" explains why: blacks are not Uncle Sam's real "children" so they do not deserve unconditional love. Moreover, it explains the fact that the "father" does not trust his "naughty children" and has to control them:

---

[7] Howard Zinn, *A People's History of the United States: 1492-Present*, p. 132.

[8] George Breitman, ed., *Malcolm X Speaks: Selected Speeches and Statements*, p. 51.

"The FBI was tappin' my telephone
I never live alone
I never walk alone
[...]
Although I live the life that of a resident
But I be knowin' the scheme that of a president."

By comparing his humble life to that of a president, *Public Enemy*'s leader shows that despite being a common citizen, he is under constant surveillance and cannot enjoy privacy. He resents control and chooses to "kick it," that is to ignore the repression. The decision not to change his life and behaviour in spite of surveillance shows his unbending stand concerning individual freedom, especially the freedom of speech. He chooses to be a free man, notwithstanding the metaphorical cage in which he is incarcerated. Chuck D voices dissatisfaction not only with the CIA and FBI but also addresses another painful issue of the African-American community, namely the racist practices of the law enforcement agencies in the USA:

"Every brothers inside so least not you forget, no
Takin' the blame is not a waste, here taste
A bit of the song so you can never be wrong
Just a bit of advice, cause we be payin' the price
'Cause every brother mans life
Is like swingin' the dice, right?"

He clearly suggests that the disproportionately large number of African-Americans in US jails is not the result of their unlawful actions but just another form of oppression used by Uncle Sam. The police are very often accused of racism by the black community, and it seems that some of these accusations are not at all unsubstantiated. In his perceptive article *Police and Thieves,* Paul Gilroy shows that police usually hold *"racist attitudes and preconceptions"*.[9] He argues that it can be partly explained by the common-sense racist ideologies which have been carefully constructed and do not represent reality but nevertheless are accepted by most of the society as "natural." Gilroy also emphasises, however, the importance of the biased training of the policemen and racism evident in police official pronouncements and analyses. He claims that

"[i]deas of black criminality appear in the struggle for legitimation, intersect with racist common sense and, in that process, provide a wealth of justifications for illegitimate, discriminatory and of course illegal police practices at the grass roots level".[10]

Like Gilroy, the rappers show how the police transform "allen blackness" into "black criminality,"[11] which justifies police brutality towards the black minority. *Public Enemy*'s reply to the violence of the state is verbal radicalism. They perform in quasi-military regalia, making constant references to militantism. The band appointed some of their members as "Ministers" of information, education and defence, following the militant *Black Panther Party*[12] which advocated a complete separation of African-Americans from white America and considered violence as necessary in order to achieve their objective. The symbolic ministers clearly inform *Public Enemy*'s audiences that both the official (white) version of history and contemporary mass media cannot be trusted: *"CIA FBI / All they tell us is lies."* Chuck D also voices a belief widespread among African-Americans by singing:

---

[9] Paul Gilroy, "Police and Thieves," in: *The Empire Strikes Back: Race and Racism in 70s Britain*, p. 145.

[10] Gilroy, "Police and Thieves", p. 145.

[11] Gilroy, "Police and Thieves", p. 145.

[12] Kellner, *Media Culture*, p. 180.

"Your CIA, you see I ain't kidding
Both King and X they got ridda' both
A story untold, true, but unknown."

The accent on your CIA emphasises the outsider status of the black community in the USA. They do not identify themselves with many American symbols and institutions and believe to inhabit a police state controlled by white oppressors. Many African-Americans realise that law enforcement agencies in the USA do not operate in black neighbourhoods to protect the community but in order to protect the interests of the white man. This is why many government institutions are alien "them" to black residents. The song clearly suggests that many African-Americans are still convinced that it was indeed the CIA and FBI that murdered Martin Luther King and Malcolm X because the white establishment could not afford to tolerate independent black leaders.

Not only do *Public Enemy's* lyrics deconstruct the racist and paternalistic ideology of white supremacy responsible for all the negative images of "blackness" held by the mainstream white society and police but they also go one step further. White supremacy is challenged by the refusal to speak the "white" language and the conscious use of the "black" version of English. Constructions like *"I be knowin'"* or *"I ain't lyin'"* represent the language used in many black communities in the USA. It is not, however, as some white racists suggest, a result of innate black inferiority and their inability to speak "proper" English but a conscious tactic of marking the difference between African-Americans and the mainstream society. By using such syntax blacks emphasise their choice to remain culturally separate from the white America.

Louder than a Bomb offers more examples of rejection of stereotypical white images of African-Americans. When Chuck D sings *"Never servin' them well, 'cause I'm an un-Tom,"* he makes reference to the famous nineteenth-century novel by Harriet Beecher Stowe *Uncle Tom's Cabin*. Uncle Tom was a slave servant devoted to his master. In black discourse (Uncle), Tom represents a meek person comfortable with the white master. The image of the black man as a "loyal Tom" persisted well into the second half of the twentieth century. Therefore Chuck D, by calling himself an "un-Tom", announces the end of subservience of the black community. *Public Enemy* thus challenges the white racist ideology which offers convenient stereotypes concerning African-Americans.

A similar stand is well illustrated by another line from the song: *"I ain't milk toast."* The reference to colour emphasises the difference between whites and blacks. There is a striking analogy to a speech by Malcolm X in which he said:

"It's just when you've got some coffee that's too black, which means it's too strong. What do you do? You integrate it with cream, you make it weak. But if you pour too much cream in it, you won't even know you ever had coffee. It used to be hot, it becomes cool. It used to be strong, it becomes weak. It used to wake you up, now it puts you to sleep".[13]

The "milk toast" is not only white but also soft. And this is the quality unacceptable for radical rappers who always portray themselves as "tough guys." They seem to believe that integration with the white society only dilutes the "black" spirit and, by doing so, erases the uniqueness of black culture. It is important to emphasise that *Public Enemy* do not only reject to conform to the stereotypes of blackness created by white ideology, but offer a range of radical solutions to the oppression of blacks and advertise an alternative "black" ideology, based primarily on Malcolm X's black nationalism. Malcolm X claimed that African-Americans should not aim at integration because white America would never let it happen. Instead of integration, he offered a radical program of complete separation of African-Americans and whites. He believed that the black community in the USA should unite and organise a revolution to gain the rights they deserved. Both Malcolm X and radical *Nation of Islam* embraced this ideology of black pride. They urged the black man not to try

[13] Breitman, *Malcolm X Speaks*, p. 16.

to accept the white way of life but to remain faithful to their own cultural traditions springing from Africa. Malcolm X claimed that blacks in the USA are Africans in America and should celebrate this difference. Chuck D clearly draws from such ideas when he refers to his fellow people using the term "black," thus emphasising the essential, race difference between his fellow people and American society at large. He also calls them "brothers," which stresses the need to unite against the common enemy, which was seen as necessity by Malcolm X, who claimed:

"We have to treat each other as brothers an sisters. We have to come together with warmth so we can develop unity and harmony that's necessary to get this problem solved ourselves."[14]

Chuck D admits: *"Our status is the saddest"* but suggests ways of improving the position of his fellow people. The solutions offered by the rappers, which often refer to some views of Malcolm X, also reflect earlier attempts at defining black identity. Both *Public Enemy* and Malcolm X seem to adopt an ideology that combines the theories of Négritude, developed in the 1930s by Léopolde Senghor and Aimé Césaire[15]. Fighting against negative stereotypes of black race, the former reconstructed "blackness" as something positive. He claimed that all people of African descent have some special characteristics, which should be embraced with pride and dignity. As to Césaire, he attempted to construct a black, pan-national identity, suggesting that what united all black men was not so much the colour of their skin but their common experience of oppression. He criticised black men for accepting the negative stereotypes concerning themselves and believed that forming a collective identity worldwide would help people of African descent liberate themselves from white domination. The idea of black power and a black pan-national movement appears in the following line from *Louder than a Bomb*:

---

[14] Breitman, *Malcolm X Speaks*, p. 7.

[15] Cf. John McLeod, *Beginning Postcolonialism*, pp. 76-81.

"No tellin' who's selllin' out— power building the nation so... / Joinin' the set, the point blank target."

Chuck D thus stigmatises the blacks who are not loyal to their community and encourages all African-Americans to unite and fight against the oppressors. He seems to believe that the combination of black pride and black power would guarantee the success of the revolution to liberate African-Americans. *Public Enemy* makes numerous references to military action and the strength of both himself and the community, such as *"The troop is always ready, I yell 'geronimo',"* or *"My posses always ready, and they're waiting in my zone."* The implication is that African-Americans have suffered long enough and are waiting to rise against the oppressors. "Geronimo," the signal to start a battle, will mark the beginning of the revolution.

Chuck D, however, also seems to suggest a metaphorical interpretation of the advocated revolution. The following lines illustrate this point:

"I am the rock hard trooper
To the bone, the bone, the bone
Full grown— consider me— stone."

The word "trooper" can be associated with the army, discipline and readiness to fight. Adding the adjective "hard", and describing himself as made of "stone", reinforces the image of an unyielding, "tough" fighter. Describing oneself as "full grown" yet again challenges the paternalistic ideology used to legitimise mistreatment. Finally, the word "rock" implies that all this belligerence is expressed through music. The line *"The rhythm is the rebel"* leaves no doubt that it is rap itself that is a means of fighting against oppression. Chuck D also explains that "D is for dangerous" and that he himself is a threat to the white establishment. He does not hesitate to speak the truth and this is why the FBI and CIA are "tappin'" his phone. When Chuck D boasts "*I'm even lethal, when I'm unarmed*," he implies that it is the very act of speaking the truth that makes him "Louder than a

Bomb," which is another openly defiant and at the same time explosive reference to military action.

Public Enemy readily rejects white supremacy and offers black pride instead. Their song, *Party for Your Right to Fight,* shows that the band promotes the ideology created by the radical African-American organisation *Nation of Islam*:

"Know who you are to be Black
To those to disagree, it causes static
For the original Black Asiatic man
Cream of the earth
And was here first
And some devils prevent this from being known."

The capitalised "Black" suggests power and pride in being dark-skinned. The "original Black Asiatic man" refers to a racist ideology created by the *Nation of Islam.* Its leaders simply superseded the ideology of white superiority with their own myths concerning race. In their theories, however, the black man is superior to the white man. It is argued that white people are devils and this is why they managed to conquer Africa, which used to be the land of kings and princes. Devils enslaved Africans but, according to this ideology of black superiority, these are blacks who are the "cream of the earth." These views clearly refer to Senghor's urgings for black pride, but seem more radical.

There appears to be, however, an essential weakness to such theories. Senghor's, Malcolm X's and *Public Enemy's* efforts to construct an ideology of black supremacy are clearly based on binary concepts of racial identity. By advocating "black pride" they do not challenge the very essence of racist theories. What they offer is a mere inversion of the existing racial hierarchy and therefore their ideology is not independent from the discourse of power imposed by the white man. Certainly, *Public Enemy* skilfully deconstructs and rejects the ideologies of white paternalism and white supremacy and thus explains the mechanisms used to keep African-Americans in inferior positions. Embracing the ideology of black superiority, however, seems immature, because it could be easily deconstructed and stigmatised with the use of the technique applied by *Public Enemy* themselves. Their ideology resembles too closely a discourse of power, which organises people into rigid communities of "us" against "them". Any theory of racial superiority seems to be based on questionable assumptions so it should be criticised no matter whether those who preach it are white or black.

WORKS CITED

Breitman, George ed., *Malcolm X Speaks: Selected Speeches and Statements.* New York: Grove Weidenfeld, 1990.

Fuchs, Lawrence H. *The American Kaleidoscope: Race, Ethnicity, and the Civic Culture.* Hannover and London: Wesleyan University Press, 1995.

Gilroy, Paul. "Police and Thieves," in: *The Empire Strikes Back: Race and Racism in 70s Britain.* ed. P. Gilroy. London and New York: Routledge, 1994.

Kellner, Douglas *Media Culture: Cultural Studies, Identity and Politics between the Modern and the Postmodern.* London and New York: Routledge, 1998.

Lawrence, Errol. "In the Abundance of Water the Fool Is Thirsty: Sociology and Black 'Pathology'," in: *The Empire Strikes Back: Race and Racism in 70s Britain*, ed. P. Gilroy London and New York: Routledge, 1994. 59-60.

McLeod, John. *Beginning Postcolonialism.* Manchester and New York: Manchester University Press, 2000.

Mohamed, Abdul R. Jan. "The Economy of Manichean Allegory," in: *The Post-colonial Studies Reader*, ed. B. Ashcroft et al. London and New York: Routledge, 1999.20-21.

Zinn, Howard. *A People's History of the United States: 1492-Present.* New York: Harper Perennial, 1995.

NOTES ON THE CONTRIBUTORS

Csapó, Csaba is a Ph.D. candidate in American literature at Eötvös Loránd University, Budapest, Hungary. At the same university, he teaches courses in English and American literature as a part-time lecturer. His research interests include English and American literature, philosophy and aesthetics. His research field is modern drama, especially the work of Tennessee Williams. He has published papers on the works of James Baldwin, Tennessee Williams, David Mamet, Jerome David Salinger as well as papers on literary theory and aesthetics in Hungary and abroad.

Detsi-Diamanti, Zoe is Lecturer at the Department of American Literature and Culture of Aristotle University, Thessaloniki, Greece. She teaches and researches in the areas of early American drama, culture, ideology, and women's studies. Her publications include articles in such journals as *American Studies*, *New England Theatre Journal*, *American Drama*, *Gramma* as well as a book on *Early American Women Dramatists, 1775-1860* (New York: Garland, 1998).

Garrigós, Cristina is Associate Professor at the University of Leon, Spain. She works on Postmodernist American Literature from a comparative perspective and has published a book on John Barth entitled *John Barth: an Author in search of Four Characters* and a number of essays on postmodernist ethnic writers and hybridization, especially on Giannina Braschi. She is also interested in the presence of Don Quixote in American Literature and has published an edition of Charlotte Lennox' s *The Female Quixote.* Currently, she is working on a book on Reading and Madness in Women writing provisionally entitled *Female Quixotism.*

Kallas, Wojciech teaches American studies and history at the Teacher Training College in Toruň, Poland. His academic interests include sociological and literary approaches to the city. He is currently working on a comparative study of the representations of the city in Wladyslaw Reymont's *The Promised Land* and Theodore Dreiser's *Sister Carrie.*
In 2003 Wojciech Kallas organized a seminar entitled *The American City: Past and Present.*

Kušnír, Jaroslav is Associate Professor at the University of Prešov, Slovakia, where he teaches such courses as American literature, English literature, Australian short story, literary theory and criticism. His research includes American postmodern fiction, Australian postmodern literature, critical reception of American, British and Australian literature in Slovakia, and literary theory and criticism. He is the author of three books: *Poetika americkej postmodernej prózy* (Richard Brautigan and Donald Barthelme)[Poetics of American Postmodern Fiction-Richard Brautigan and Donald Barthelme].Prešov: Impreso, 2001; *American Fiction: Modernism-Postmodernism, Popular Culture, and Metafiction.*Stuttgart: Ibidem Verlag, 2005; and *Australian Literature in Contexts.* Banská Bystrica: Trian, 2003 and 2004.

Ni, Pi-hua is currently the Director of General Education Center and Associate Professor in the Department of Western Languages and Literature at National University of Kaohsiung, Taiwan. A grantee of the 2000 Fulbright American Studies Institute on Contemporary American Literature, Ni has worked on research projects such as *On Postmodern Parody: The Case of Donald Barthelme, Game, Reality and History in Postmodern Fiction: The Case of John Barth* and *Pen(is) in John Barth's Postmodern Fiction: From Patriarchal to Androgynous Narrative Paradigm.* Her publications include *Game, Reality and History in Postmodern Fiction: On the Contribution of Postmodern Fiction*, *On Postmodern Parody: The Case of Donald Barthelme*; *[(Historiographic)Meta] Fiction: On Linda Hutcheon's 'Historiographic*

Metafiction', The History/Fiction Borderline Transgressed: On the Multiple Subversive Narratives in The White Hotel and other essays on John Barth.

Oha, Obododimma teaches stylistics at the Department of English at the University of Ibadan, Nigeria. He has published a number of papers in journals such as *Mosaic, Mattoid, Mots Pluriels, American Drama, Philosophy and Social Action, African Anthropology,* and *CONTEXT*. He is also a poet and playwright.

Peprník, Michal is Associate Professor at the Palacký University at Olomouc, Czech Republic, where he teaches the courses such as American literature, literary theory and criticism, the American West. His research includes modern literary theory and criticism, American fiction of the 19th century, Modern American fiction and Scottish literature. He is an author of *Směry literární interpretace XX. století— texty, komentáře* [*Approaches to Literary Interpretation in the 20th Century: Texts and Comments*]. Olomouc: UP,2000; and *Metamorfóza jako kulturní metafora: James Hogg, R. L. Stevenson a George Mac Donald [Metamorphosis as a Cultural Metaphor: James Hogg, R. L. Stevenson and George MacDonald]*. Olomouc: Palacký University, 2003.

Pokrivčák, Anton is Associate Professor and currently a Vice-Dean for Foreign Affairs at the Faculty of Arts, Constantine the Philosopher University in Nitra, Slovakia. At the same institution, he is an instructor teaching such courses as introduction to the study of literature, survey of American literature, literary criticism, and postmodern critical theory. His research includes contemporary and 19th century American fiction, literary theory and criticism and contemporary American fiction. He is an author of *History of Great Britain and the USA (An Introduction)* Nitra: Pedagogická fakulta, 1990; *Literatúra a bytie [Literature and Being]* Nitra: UKF, 1997; Americká imaginácia *[American Imagination]* Nitra: UKF, 2005.

Stauffer, John is the John L. Loeb Associate Professor of the Humanities at Harvard University. He received his Ph.D. in American Studies at Yale University in 1999, and won the Ralph Henry Gabriel Prize for the best dissertation in American Studies from the American Studies Association. His first book, *The Black Hearts of Men: Radical Abolitionists and the Transformation of Race* (Harvard University Press, 2002) was the co-winner of the 2002 Frederick Douglass Book Prize from the Gilder Lehrman Institute; winner of the Avery Craven Book Prize from the OAH; and the Lincoln Prize runner-up. He is the editor of Frederick Douglass' *My Bondage and My Freedom* for the Modern Library; is editing a collection of John Brown's writings; co-editing (with Tim McCarthy) a collection of abolitionist essays; and is at work on a new book, *By the Love of Comrades: Interracial Friendships and American Race Relations.*

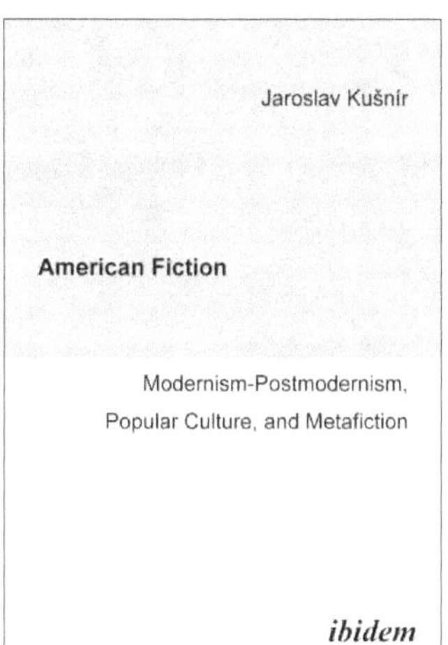

Jaroslav Kušnír

American Fiction

Modernism-Postmodernism,
Popular Culture, and Metafiction

ISBN 3-89821-514-8
218 S., Paperback, € 24,90

Jaroslav Kušnír's book *American Fiction: Modernism-Postmodernism, Popular Culture, and Metafiction* is a sequel to his previous study on American postmodern fiction entitled *Poetika americkej postmodernej prózy: Richard Brautigan and Donald Barthelme* [*Poetics of American Fiction: Richard Brautigan and Donald Barthelme*]. Prešov: Impreso, 2001. It explores various aspects of American postmodernist fiction as manifested in the works by Richard Brautigan, Donald Barthelme and other American postmodernist authors such as Robert Coover, E. L. Doctorow, Kurt Vonnegut and Paul Auster. Analyzing various short stories and novels, the author shows differences between modernist and postmodernist literature in the works of Donald Barthelme; the way postmodern parodies of popular literary genres give a critique of some aspects of American cultural identity and experience (the American Dream, individualism, consumerism); and he also shows different ways postmodern authors such as Robert Coover, Kurt Vonnegut and Paul Auster create metafictional effect as one of the most significant aspects of postmodern literature.

The author: Jaroslav Kušnír is the Associate Professor at the University of Prešov, Slovakia, where he teaches such courses as American literature, British literature, Australian short story, literary theory and criticism. His research includes American postmodern and contemporary fiction, Australian postmodern fiction, and critical reception of American, British and Australian literature in Slovakia. He is the author of *Poetika americkej postmodernej prózy (Richard Brautigan and Donald Barthelme)*[*Poetics of American Postmodern Fiction: Richard Brautigan and Donald Barthelme*]. Prešov: Impreso, 2001; and *Australian Literature in Contexts*. Banská Bystrica: Trian, 2003.

ibidem-Verlag • Melchiorstr. 15 • 70439 Stuttgart • Tel.: 0711/9807954 • Fax: 0711/8001889
ibidem@ibidem-verlag.de

ibidem-Verlag
Melchiorstr. 15
D-70439 Stuttgart

info@ibidem-verlag.de

www.ibidem-verlag.de
www.edition-noema.de
www.autorenbetreuung.de

www.ingramcontent.com/pod-product-compliance
Lightning Source LLC
LaVergne TN
LVHW020715110826
845149LV00012B/2274

* 9 7 8 3 8 9 8 2 1 5 1 3 8 *